*On The Bright Side*

*On The Bright Side*

For more information please visit: www.TheReadingTutor.org

GabrielPress: www.GabrielPressUSA.com

Chicago, Il. 60655

The author and publisher have taken reasonable precautions in the preparation of this book and believe the information presented in the book is accurate as of the date it was written. However, neither the author nor the publisher assumes any responsibility for any errors or omissions. The author and publisher specifically disclaim any liability resulting from the use or application of the information contained in this book, and the information is not intended to serve as legal, financial or other professional advice related to individual situations. The views and opinions herein are solely the author's.

On the Bright Side Copyright @ 2015 by Veronica Jennings McCarthy

All rights reserved. No part of this book may be reproduced or utilized in any form or by any means, electronic or mechanical, including photocopying, recording, or by any information storage and retrieval system, without permission in writing from the author, except for the inclusion of brief quotations in a review.

ISBN: 978-1-941296-03-5

Printed and bound in the United States of America

*The battle is won in the silence of your soul, my dearest friend.*

St Gertrude

I dedicate this book to my husband, Brian J. McCarthy, who has consistently worked so hard over all these years and whose help I inevitably rely upon at some point to complete every new "idea" I have.

And also to Robert L. Montgomery who has over his lifetime embodied all that is contained in this book and continues to inspire others to do the same.

## Introduction

The idea for this book came about during a very difficult time in my life. My father was dying and most days did not recognize me; my doctor had called to inform me that my chronic cough was not a result of low iron like I thought but the result of a serious disease that had damaged my heart and lungs; my business hit an extremely low point and I was not making enough money which was strongly impacting my family; people that I thought were my friends turned out not to be; and I was in the process of completing very expensive and painful dental surgeries. I was financially, mentally and spiritually drained. This was one of the lowest points in my life.

I was leaving my bedroom one morning and I saw the crucifix on the wall out of the corner of my eye. I felt drawn to sit down and rest for a minute. I sat on the couch and stared at the crucifix thinking how life could be so difficult. Then my hand touched a small notebook that was on the couch.

The notebook contained notes I had taken from several books I had read. Over the past couple of years I wrote down anything from a book I was reading that inspired me, and that I wanted to remember.

I began reading the notes, message by message, page after page. Little by little the feeling of despondency lifted and was replaced by the feeling that not only could I handle all this, I could also choose to be happy. The choice was mine on how I wanted to live my life.

I gave a lot of thought to what I wanted to accomplish and I made a list of all my goals. Then I began working on my goals, one by one. This all began by reading the notes I took from the writings of all these beautiful and inspired authors.

One of my goals was to share what inspired me with others. Everyone has low points in their life, that is a given. What we do during our low points is really the key to our future. Charles Haanel wrote, "If you wish to change conditions you must change yourself. Your whims, your wishes, your fancies, your ambitions may be thwarted at every step, but your inmost thoughts will find expression just as certainly as the plant springs from the seed."

I took a look at my innermost thoughts at this time and they weren't pretty. I was choosing to look at what was bad in my life, not what was good. Haanel wrote that Carlyle hated all that was bad and Emerson loved all that was good. Carlyle's life was very difficult while Emerson's life was peaceful and full of joy.

We choose our life just as we choose our thoughts and make our choices.

Use this little book to become inspired and begin the life you always wanted to live. Open it to any page and start reading the thoughts that inspired countless people before you and me. If a particular author resonates with you, look up and read the books he wrote. His work is bound to inspire you and direct you even more.

I sincerely hope and pray that each person who reads these writings will be as encouraged as I was to face each day with confidence, joy and peace, for there is so much that is good in this world.

You have power over your mind, not outside events.

Realize this, and you will find strength.

Marcus Aurelius

### Thoughts are Things

Thoughts are things and things are thoughts.

What one thinks, materializes.

What you think – you are.

Charles Haanel

As a man thinketh in his heart, so is he.

James Allen

Thought is creative energy and will automatically correlate with its object and bring it into manifestation because thought is a spiritual energy or vibration.

Think about what you want and how to get it.

Charles Haanel

The only thing that stands between a man and what he wants from life is often merely the will to try it and the faith to believe that it is possible.

Richard Devos

Happiness is the harvest of a quiet mind. Anchor your thought on peace, poise, security and divine guidance and your mind will be productive of happiness.

Joseph Murphy

In the last analysis, man is just what he thinks himself to be; he is big in capacity if he thinks big thoughts; he is small if he thinks small thoughts. He will attract to himself what he thinks most about. He can learn to govern his own destiny when he learns to control his thoughts…Believing; thinking into Mind each day that which is wished to be returned; eliminating negative thoughts; thinking positive thoughts; giving thanks to the Spirit of Life that it is so trusting always in the Higher Law; never arguing with one's self or with others; these are the steps which, when followed, will bring us to where we shall not have to ask if it be true, for, having demonstrated, <u>we shall know</u>. The seed that falls into the ground shall bear fruit of its own kind, and nothing shall hinder it.

Ernest Holmes

Practice resting yourself in God. Practice depending on Him for His support and power. Believe He is giving it to you now. Yield yourself to it – let it flow through you. Take three deep breaths. Relax.

Norman Vincent Peale

I am with My children. My presence is silent but constant. I am directing many of the seemingly unimportant events in your lives, so that My will can be accomplished. My children are practicing faith, and that pleases Me. But My protection is so great that My children could have an infinite amount of faith in Me and still more would be justified. My faithful ones, who are struggling to serve Me and be holy, please trust Me for I am with you. I have pledged My protection to you and I will not leave you vulnerable. Offer Me small little prayers when you are frightened or unsure and I will place My calming hands upon you, steadying and reassuring you. You will look back at this time of service to Me and you will be so grateful that you said 'yes' to your God. My children, you will look upon so many souls sharing eternity with you who would be absent if not for your service. Can you imagine the joy you will share with these souls? So be brave and continue in My service, walking the path I have illuminated before you. It is there you will find your peace and your key to eternity. For today, I want to warn you about a snare or a trap. My children often want to do big things for Me, and truly, big things are necessary and big things will be asked of you. But your holiness lies in the small, dear soul. It is in the small unseen tasks and duties that I whisper to your soul, that I mold a bit here reform a bit there, You do not feel these changes because they are so subtle, but changes occur, My child, in the small things. So do not begrudge Me the mundane. Complete small, humble acts with love and patience so that I may do My work in your soul as quickly as possible. Yes, we are going to save many souls, and bring the world back to the light, but we are going to do that one soul at a time. Right now, I am starting with you. So give yourself to Me that I may change the world. Together you and I must perfect your beautiful soul, insuring that it reaches its fullest potential, both here and in Heaven. Do you trust Me, My child? Trust can be difficult, but this is one time when you can step out in complete trust and confidence because I will not let you fall. I am here, ready to save you. I have waited for this day, My child, for so long. My heart aches with love for you and watching your read these words creates an even stronger love in My heart. I will take care of you and you can close your eyes and rest in My heart. You have suffered because of the distance between us. Often you did not know where the pain originated, but I assure you, the pain began when you turned away from Me. Our standards must be high now, as I desire your happiness. I want you to remain in My heart where I place you today. I will help, My dear child. You are infinitely precious to Me and if you show Me the smallest desire, I can keep you firmly joined to Me, despite the winds that try to tear you away. Have every confidence that the smallest bit of faith will be rewarded in these days of difficulty. Heaven is united with earth in this mission of salvation for souls. All assistance is available to each soul who seeks to be saved. Be at peace, now, My little soul. I am holding you tightly.

Jesus

as given to Anne, a lay apostle

Imagination is the process of imaging these things in or on your mind, and this process is nature's method of creation.

… you must think of the result, not upon how it is accomplished. When you become familiar with the operation of this law, you will have found the secret of success, of health, of prosperity, of happiness, and of popularity. You will have discovered a law that is as dependable as the law of gravitation.

If you think or concentrate along any particular line, you start a train of causation and if your thought is sufficiently concentrated and kept continuously in mind, what happens?

There is only one thing that can occur. Whatever the vision you have, the imagination you have, the image is accepted by the Universal Intelligence, expressing through the cells of your physical body and environment, and these cells send out their calls into the great formless energy everywhere around you for the material that corresponds with the image and harmonizes in its vibration with it and whether the image is for success along any particular line or fear of a particular thing, you call the atoms from out of the formless energy which make for the success or the thing you fear - you relate with conditions necessary to bring into manifestation the thing you desire or the thing you fear.

Charles Haanel

Whatever you believe with conviction becomes your reality.

Brian Tracy

*On The Bright Side*

I am whole, perfect, strong, powerful, loving, harmonious, prosperous and happy. These are creative words.

Charles Haanel

The rough is only mental. I think Victory – I get Victory.

The rough is only mental. It is rough because you think it is. In your mind you have decided that here is an obstacle which will cause you difficulty. The power to overcome this obstacle is in your mind. If you visualize yourself succeeding, believing you can do it, your mind will transfer flexibility, rhythm and power to you. Remember, the rough is only mental.

Norman Vincent Peale

Try not to become a person of success, but rather try to become a person of value.

Albert Einstein

Your success comes from what you do with the knowledge you acquire.

Take what you know and do something with it.

Action

I expect the best and with God's help I will attain the best. Tap #1: Repetition, reiteration of the <u>desire</u> of what you want. Tap #2: Get a perfect detailed picture of the thing you want and use repetition and reiteration. TNT = a mental image of what you want and the faith that you can and will get it. The realization that what you picture in your mind, if you picture it clearly and confidently and persistently enough, will eventually come to pass in your life!

Create what happens to you by correct thinking.

Everything in the universe is electro-magnetic in nature. The laws of attraction and repulsion operate electromagnetically; that when you assume a positive or negative attitude of mind, you get a positive or negative result; there is no such thing as an accident. Everything happens in accordance with the laws of cause and effect.

You have to think big to be big.

Picture what you want.

If you believe it – it is so. As a man thinketh in his heart so is he. Faith.

Believe in yourself.


I know it. I believe it and it is so.

What have you been seeking all these years?

What were you taught?

What did you learn?

Where have you been?

Where are you going?

Claude M. Bristol

*On The Bright Side*

A man's true greatness lies in the consciousness of an honest purpose in life, founded on a just estimate of himself and everything else, on frequent self-examinations, and a steady obedience to the rule which he knows to be right, without troubling himself about what others may think or say, or whether they do or do not do that which he thinks and says and does.

Marcus Aurelius

You become what you think about all day long.  (be positive – think success)

Ralph Waldo Emerson

You will be judged by what's in your heart towards others –

Not what's in their heart towards you.

Robert Montgomery paraphrasing unknown author

You do not believe what you see. You see what you already believe.

Brian Tracy

Fear is really nothing other than a self-limiting reaction that we've always mistaken for a shield of self-protection. It's time to let it go, which you can do anytime you want. Here's how: Just dare to proceed, even while being afraid.

Guy Finley

It is true that some of the time the experience of our humanity is that of loneliness and pain, discouragement and sadness, and above all, isolation, even from those closest to us. It is said that every man is an island and I believe that there is truth to this. Still, I think God requires periodic isolation in order to fix each man's eyes more firmly on Him. Some lessons we must learn alone. Period. Humanity cannot breach this type of isolation.

If we accept that feeling abandoned in our pain and feeling that nobody understands our pain is necessary for us to grow in holiness, we will be less afraid of these periods. We will lament less. We should view these times as invitations from the Trinity to rest our souls in the place of the divine will, where we are surrounded by saints and angels.

Anne, a lay apostle

Faith is to believe what you do not see;

the reward of this faith is to see what you believe.

St. Augustine

## The ABC's of Success

Whatever the mind of man can **C**onceive and **B**elieve it can **A**chieve.

Napoleon Hill

What makes someone a success?

Belief, Faith – only that, and the ability of a staunch believer to pass it on to the other fellow.

All big things are started by one person, one believer. It makes no difference where they got the idea originally. All great inventions are the outgrowth of the whole scheme – Faith, Faith – belief in yourself, your ideas.

Every community drive, every forward movement, everything worthwhile succeeds because some one person has Faith, and is able to pass it on and on. Meditate on this.

Don't envy. Do.

Everything that anyone has ever done constructively has been done from within himself. Every one of us, if put on the right track can accomplish what he or she is after by keeping before him or her my own expression: 'If you believe, it's so' and adopting the old adage, 'where there's a will there's a way.'

Get that will power, that Faith – that Belief working every minute of the day – 24 hours a day – 7 days a week – 365 days a year. And I promise you if it's done you will leave people around you in the progress you make as rapidly as high frequency electrical discharges oscillate through the ether.

…it's the repetition that ultimately makes its impression on the human mind,

tap, tap, tap.

Claude M. Bristol

A man who is self-reliant, positive optimistic, and undertakes his work with the assurance of success magnetizes his condition. He draws to himself the creative power of the universe.

It is indeed a fact that the person who thinks with positive self-reliance and optimism does magnetize his condition and releases power to attain his goal. So expect the best at all times. Nurture it, concentrate on it, emphasize it, visualize it, prayerize it, surround it with faith. Expect the best and spiritually created mind power, aided by God Power, will produce the best.

Norman Vincent Peale

If you can get a definite detailed picture in your conscious mind by using this process of reiteration or repetition and make the subconscious mind click, you have at your command a power that astounds.

The impulses come when you get up against it. You who have been there know what you had to rely on in times of acute pressure, and whether or not you heard a little voice from within. Where are you going?

There can be no gainsaying that once you have made up your mind to do a thing it will be done. But the trouble with most of us is that we side step, vacillate and seldom make up our minds to what we want or determine clearly the road on which we wish to travel.

Claude M. Bristol

Success is goals

Write down your goals, make plans to achieve them, and work on your plans every single day.

Brian Tracy

All daydreams and wishes would become realities if we kept them constantly before us – <u>put fear behind</u> – shoved away all reservations, ifs, ands, and buts. Again, a lot of us think we know what we want when; as a matter of fact, we don't. This sounds paradoxical, but if each person knew what he wanted, he would get it provided he had the will power, the stamina, the dynamic force, the fight to go after it.

Therefore, the first thing to do is get that spirit of determination. That may be obtained by constantly saying to yourself:

I Will, I Will, I Will, I Will I Will,

and believe it.

Now if you have the desire the foundation is laid. Get a perfect detailed picture of the exact thing, or things, you wish…No matter what you are after under this system, you can have it provided the desire is definite and positive.

When you have the picture firmly in mind begin using the tap, tap system…It is going to be the repetition, the reiteration of that picture upon the subconscious mind that will cause the little voice from within to speak and point out to you accurately and scientifically how you are to proceed to get what you want. And when you move, <u>all obstacles will become phantoms</u>.

The idea is to keep the picture or pictures before you constantly. As an aid in the visualization of the things you want, and to keep them uppermost in your mind, write a word picture of them on several cards. Keep them always in your possession and look at them as frequently as possible bearing in mind, the more often you glance at them, the firmer becomes the impression upon your consciousness. Pin one card on the mirror for the morning. Look at the cards morning, breakfast, lunch, dinner, and before you sleep. Permit the details to increase. Look in the mirror and tell yourself where you are going.

When you get the pictures clearly defined do not for an instant permit them to escape you. Hold them with bands of steel.

Claude M. Bristol

*On The Bright Side*

So use all that is called Fortune. Most men gamble with her and gain all, and lose all, as her wheel rolls. But do thou leave as unlawful these winnings, and deal with Cause and Effect, the chancellors of God. In the Will work and acquire, and thou hast chained the wheel of chance, and shall sit hereafter out of fear from her rotations…Nothing can bring you peace but yourself. Nothing can bring you peace but the triumph of principles.

Ralph Waldo Emerson

You are not what you think you are,

But, what you think, you are.

I am in charge of my life. I am responsible for the outcome.

Brian Tracy

Of all the sad words of tongue and pen, the saddest are these; it might have been.

John Whittier

YOU are engineered for greatness

And

designed for success.

Brian Tracy

*On The Bright Side*

Affirm the good and the bad will vanish.

Joseph Murphy

Thoughts are causes and conditions are effects.

James Allen

Go thy way; and as thou hast believed, so be it done unto thee.

Matthew 8:13

Every success has been accomplished by persistent concentration upon the object in view.

Charles Haanel

What one thing do you desire above everything else in life?

Whatever it is, you can have it. Whatever you desire, wholeheartedly, with singleness of purpose – you can have. But the first and all-important essential is to know what this one thing is. Before you can win your heart's desire, you've got to get clearly fixed in your mind's eye what it is that you want.

In the realm of mind, the realm in which is all practical power, you can possess what you want at once. You have but to claim it, to visualize it, to bring it into actuality – and it is yours for the taking. For the Genie-of-your-Mind can give you power over circumstances. Health, happiness and prosperity.

And all you need to put it to work is an earnest, intense desire.

Robert Collier

Act yourself into feeling a certain way.

Think successful – Act successful – Dress successful – Be successful.

Everything you say and do has to be consistent with your new attitude of success.

Think Happy – Act Happy – Be Happy

Think Kindness – Act with Kindness – Become Kind

You might not be born successful, happy, kind … but at any time in your life you can choose to be any quality you want to be.

Choose it – think it – visualize yourself as already possessing the quality – act as if you have this quality – become the person with this quality.

Look within,

within is the fountain of good and it will ever bubble up,

if thou wilt ever dig

Ancient Saying

What is the reality? Look at where you are and where you need to go…

Stop blaming

Think positive

Be positive

Accept people the way they are

Accept personal responsibility – For everything



Be more positive

Be more consistent

Be more confident

Have Faith

Do the work



Look out at your environment right now. Do you like what you see? Are you where you want to be? Your thoughts placed you here. If you don't like what you see, change your thoughts. Plan and visualize what you want to see. Write it down on paper. Commit yourself to attaining this goal. What can you do right now to begin the journey towards your goal? Take the first step

The law is that thought is an active vital form of dynamic energy which has the power to correlate with its object and bring it out of the invisible substance from which all things are created into the visible or objective world.

This is the law by which and through which all things come into manifestation; it is the Master Key by which you are admitted into the Secret Place of the Most High and are "given dominion over all things."

With an understanding of this law you may "decree a thing and it shall be established unto thee."

Charles Haanel

…but the Father that dwelleth in me, He doeth the works.

John 14:10

The time you put in aimlessly dreaming and wishing would accomplish marvels if it were concentrated on one definite object. If you have ever taken a magnifying glass and let the sun's rays play through it on some object, you know that as long as the rays were scattered they accomplished nothing. But focus them on one tiny spot and see how quickly they start something. It is the same way with your mind. You've got to concentrate on one idea at a time.

Robert Collier

*On The Bright Side*

To have more, you must first Be more.

Goethe

Study, learn, work. Develop a keenness of observation. Step on the gas. Become alive for yourself, and you'll pass it on to the other fellow. Get confidence, enthusiasm and you'll set up like vibrations all around you and that's the theory of all life – as old as the world itself. Like begets like – a laugh brings a laugh – a good deed calls for a good deed – riches begets riches, love, love - and so on.

And while there is no point to going around hitting everybody on the nose just to start something, always remember it is poor business to let your self be put on the defensive as that is a negative sign.

The person who won't be licked, can't be licked.

If you are taken unawares and suddenly put on the defensive, snap out of it. Take the offensive because if you remain on the defensive, you are beaten.

Reiteration – Repetition

Keeping uppermost in your mind all the time what you want and which positive thoughts, in turn, are passed on to the subconscious mind – the wonder thing. Think health, wealth and happiness and they will all be yours.

It cannot be otherwise.

Think affirmatively, and the first thing you know your aches, worries and troubles will disappear.

Claude M. Bristol

*On The Bright Side*

The thoughts you think and the things you do NOW will determine your future destination. Are you on the right course to get from where you are now to where you really want to be?

William Clement Stone

Direct your thoughts,

Control your emotions.

Ordain your destiny.

You CAN be what you want to be.

Napoleon Hill

If thou are pained by any external thing, it is not this thing which disturbs thee, but thy own judgement about it. And it is in thy power to wipe out this judgement now. But if anything in thy own disposition gives thee pain, who hinders thee from correcting thy opinion?

Philosophy of the Ages

Compare yourself to the gears of your automobile. In reverse place all fears, worries, troubles, aches and pains. And when things go wrong simply put on the brakes, idle your engine until you can clearly see the road ahead (the fright train has passed, gates are up.)

In high gear is everything you desire, health, wealth, happiness – success. No power in the world except your hand can put the gears of your automobile in reverse. If your own gears get in reverse remember you alone put them there. Erect a steel wall on the right side of the reverse gear, close the doors of yesterday and you will have to shift from low into high and stay there.

Successful people are those who made themselves and not what others made them. After all, there are only two ways to move; forward and backward. Why not forward?

Ascertain exactly what you want, and use the mechanics given, and you will discover more gates open for you than you ever dreamed existed. A light will dawn upon you and you will see clearly ahead how to achieve what you are after. The same principles, the same methods can be successfully applied to any line. The ability to accomplish anything in a convincing fashion depends entirely upon the degree of expert knowledge, which you possess coupled with that intensity of purpose. Read and study. Practice, practice, tap, tap, tap.

Claude M. Bristol

*On The Bright Side*

The little voice spoke - just like it always does when you make up your mind what you want and when you go after it.


If your little inner voice suggests that you ask for something, do not be backward about asking. You have nothing to fear. The other person will never help unless he knows your wishes, so you must ask. Accept the theory advanced here in and practice intelligently and the voice will speak… You will get results – all will be yours.


The fault, dear Brutus, is not in our stars, but in ourselves that we are underlings.

William Shakespeare


If you are timid, backward, in a rut, and an underling, it is because of yourself. Blame not the stars. Blame not society. Blame not the world. Blame yourself. Again I say, change gears. Put them in high and begin to move.


… "tap" yourself, upward or downward – dependent on whether you have depressed or constructive thoughts.


Fill your mind with creative thoughts and then act as the ideas come to you. Remember, every thought, kept ever constant, leads to action.

Claude M. Bristol

The richest mine in the world is the one within yourself,

begin today to develop it.

Francis T. Miller

You are what you think yourself to be.

Happiness is a state of mind. The kingdom is within. The real you is a higher you, a greater power that resides within you or is available to you whenever you ask or seek. The fact is that it's your birthright to manifest the glory of the incredible you.

So the first fundamental is you. The power resides with you, and no one else can do it for you. Your thoughts are reflections of your expectations. What has been sown in your subconscious mind is what you reap. Doubt produces failure, fear yields anger, and belief in limitations is the greatest of all self-fulfilling prophecies.

The thoughts we have reveal the beliefs we have about ourselves. Listen to how you talk to yourself. Is the language from the inside reflecting optimism, or is it filled with negative and self-limiting ideas?

Eldon Taylor

Negative self-limiting ideas will cause resistance to your success.

*On The Bright Side*

The things that matter most must never be at the mercy

of the things that matter least.

Goethe

What matters most to you?

When fear rules the will, nothing can be done, but when a man casts fear out of his mind the world becomes his oyster. To lose a bit of money is nothing but to lose hope – to lose nerve and ambition – that is what makes men cripples.

Herbert N. Casson

Hold your goal before you. Everything else will take care of itself.

Act as though it were impossible to fail.

The law is that your financial return will be in direct proportion to your service.

Be of service; build, work, dream, create, inspire. No man can get rich himself unless he enriches others.

Earl Nightingale

Forgive and let go. The power to grow resides in forgiveness. Letting go will set us free. As long as you shift responsibility by blaming someone or something for who and what you are, you remove from yourself the power to be anything other than partial and incomplete.

Eldon Taylor

All behavior is the result of choice.

What are you choosing?

The more you give of yourself with no expectation of return, the more that will come back to you from the most unexpected sources.

Quoted by Brian Tracy

Every day in every way I am getting better and better.

Emile Coue

*On The Bright Side*

Whatever is impressed, is expressed.

Aristotle

Think → Do

I know it, I believe it, and it is so.

I am the master of my fate, I am the captain of my soul.

Henley

Each step **into** what you think you can't do is one step **further away** from that nature which wants you to think that circles actually go somewhere.

Learn to ask for a happy, new life, by refusing to relive what's been tearing at you.

True strength is the flower of Wisdom, but its seed is action.

Never again look for a way out of any anxious condition. Look instead for a way to see through it.

Guy Finley

Children of the world, look toward the light. Raise your eyes to all that is goodness. I come to you with joy and celebration. The time for mourning is past because God has taken His children back to His breast, never to be parted. This world, your world, has suffered. Sin obscured the light until children began to doubt the very existence of God. This will never be allowed to happen again. God, in all His omniscience, allowed mankind to direct itself and direct the course of humanity so that he could see the fruits of separation from heaven. Children, with all of the wisdom of heaven, you can now see the level of darkness that settled in ever growing layers upon the world. Prophets from even one hundred years ago could never have imagined such evil. They could not fathom the depravity that would be accepted by men of the future. The enemies of heaven have persuaded humanity that much of this evil is good. We have visited those absurdities and need dwell no longer on them because I have come. I am leading you to the light that never changes. There will not be a new light tomorrow. God is and will be. He is eternal. His laws have no need of adaptation to new generations, children, because they are the guides for all humans, given the inclinations that can draw man from God. Women of the world, rejoice. Your salvation is at hand. Your children's children will be joyful followers of the light. Have no fear that your world spins out of control. God's sustaining hand is directing all. Pray with confidence that all has been allowed for the triumph of heaven and of heaven's children. If you experience grief, know that I will wipe away every tear. You will be comforted with divine comfort if you ask Me. Heaven and earth are joined together to usher in the New Time. All is well, dear humanity. All is well.

Jesus

as given to Anne, a lay apostle

I give greetings to My children on this earth. It is I, your Father in heaven, who speaks to you. My children, you are participating in a time of change. The saints in heaven only wished they could have lived in this time. It is similar to the time when Jesus was born in Bethlehem. You might say the world is with child again because the world is awaiting the return of the Savior. Jesus loves this world and Jesus loves each one of you tenderly. I will not even discuss the love that I hold for each of you because it is understood that a Creator, when He creates something as precious and perfect as each one of you, loves the created. You are the created, children of heaven. You did not accidentally arrive on earth due to a series of biological events. This is nonsense. The biological event that was your birth caused all of heaven to let out their breath in expectation of your time in the world. I created you to bring My Kingdom on earth that much closer to the return of My Son. You are to participate in this joyous process. You must ask Me, your God, what plan I have for your participation. Some will reject Me, of course. I am well used to that during this age of disobedience. So perhaps I might ask you to serve Me in all love and allegiance to compensate for those who reject Me. Will you do that for Me, My little souls? Please have no fears. Understand that the Father wills these changes on earth so that the Son will be welcomed in the hearts of those remaining. We do not manifest as a poor boy in the stable. We manifest as the King of Creation. My Son is your God. I am your God. Our Spirit flows through your world in such a way today that no one can deny the heavenly times. The enemy will deny Our Spirit. But you expect that dear ones. That denial detracts in no way from truth. Truth flows right over the enemy despite the feeble objections of evil. I, the God of All Creation, can slap down and destroy evil with a glance. I allow a certain amount of evil to co-exist because My children can then discern between light and darkness, in the same way a child is taught to discriminate between cold and hot. Children, if you desire to blame Me for the state of the world, your ancestors in heaven will bow their heads in disappointment. Do not be so ridiculous. I do not will catastrophe upon My children. I do allow a certain amount of upheaval so that attention will be focused away from the ever present diversion of material goods. In line with this goal, I will begin to remove many material comforts. Consider this a liberating experience, earthly creatures. Your losses on earth are nothing in comparison to the loss you will experience if you choose darkness. Be humble and accepting in everything and together We will prepare the world for the return of My Son.

God the Father

as given to Anne, a lay apostle

The fact is it is your birth right to manifest the glory of the incredible you. You absolutely have the power and ability to experience all the bounties of life, to experience many literal miracles in your life for you yourself are a miracle and all that you are or can ever be is a gift.

The world is a mirror,

for the principle function of the world is to provide us the opportunity to learn.

What we like least in another is, almost always,

a reflection of something in ourselves.

Eldon Taylor

You must be so resolute and determined,

so convinced of your ultimate success,

that nothing can stop you.

Positive knowing –

absolutely know and believe.

Brian Tracy

I remember a time during one of life's tragedies when a strange woman ministered to me. I was crouched against a wall in front of a hospital, terribly frightened as a family member was near death because of a serious accident. It was dark and a woman walked by me, hurrying along. I barely noticed her. She stopped suddenly, turned back and approached me with the greatest confidence.

"What's wrong, Honey?" she asked.

Startled, I told her in a few sentences. I was not interested in conversation, to be honest, as I had been talked to death in the immediate past few days.

"Well," she said, letting her breath out in a huge sigh, "You need Jesus Christ as sure as I'm standing here. I just knew He was asking me to stop and minister to you."

With that she dropped her purse and shopping bags. Now, she was clearly not Catholic. I am Catholic and as a Catholic I was raised to pray quietly in form. This woman was a big woman with a big wild hat and brightly-colored clothes. Even her bags were wildly colored. I couldn't imagine why she was dropping everything there on the street in sub-zero temperatures. She made me extremely nervous.

I remained with my back to the wall. She put her hands over my head and let heaven have it.

"Jesus Christ," said she in a strong, loud voice, "I know You're there and I know You're listening. This poor little thing is looking like she's all alone down here and I don't like it, not one little bit. I ain't going nowhere, Lord, till You give this child the grace she has a right to expect from You. You hear me, Jesus. I know You do. Look how cold she is, Lord. Look how scared she looks. She believes in You, Jesus and she shouldn't look so cold and scared. We need help right now."

She paused in the silence. The people gathering around us were also silent. Nervous laughter spilled out of me.

"Help us, Jesus. Help us right now." She waited again. "I'm still here, Lord. I'm not leaving until You help her."

At that point, I joined her in prayer.

Suddenly, waves of grace came down on me. All my fears left as strength poured into me. The woman put her hands on my head and warmth flowed from them. I felt such love and peace. I looked up at her in surprise and her beautiful warm brown eyes looked back at me. "He was here all the time, Honey," she said gently. "He wouldn't leave you. You just couldn't feel him."

With that she picked up her bags and purse and left, leaving me hugely consoled. I think of her so often over the years. This woman was paying attention. She looked tired and she walked as though her feet hurt and yet she stopped and loved me, a stranger who was nothing to her. This beautiful apostle was paying attention to Jesus.

Anne, a lay apostle

Any thought, plan, goal or idea held continuously in the conscious mind must inevitable be brought into reality by the superconscious mind.

Your superconscious mind is stimulated by clear, written, specific goals, intensely desired, visualized regularly, and constantly worked towards.

Look for the good in every situation.

Concentrate and work on achieving your goal. Think about it, talk about it, write it, rewrite it and review it every single day.

If you get an inner urge, act quickly. This is often time dated information.

Don't merely dream, but create!

Brian Tracy

*On The Bright Side*

My children in this changing world, I want you to know that I am with you. I tell you this often in many ways, because if you give consideration to the thought that your God is present in all that occurs, you will not feel frightened. How can a soul be afraid when the all-powerful, all-knowing Father is present, watching each situation, and through each situation, bringing about the best possible outcome for that soul? You do not see Me, it is true, but again I make reference to the wind, which makes its presence felt in its effects. I am that way also. You know I am present by the effect I have on you, on the situation where I am called in, and on the souls who respond to My presence within you. You see, My children in the world, I use each one of you to bring Me and present Me to others. If you are respectful of Me, if you acknowledge My dominion over you and your world, I am with you. In this way, I can be brought everywhere, I can be present to any soul who is with you. I can manifest Myself in many ways. I manifest Myself in your patience. I manifest Myself in your love for another when you ordinarily would find it difficult to love that person. I am present in your smile, in your speech, and I am present in your decisions, which is very important. So you do not see Me, it is true, but you will feel the difference if you go either from serving Me to not serving Me, or from not serving Me to serving Me. Serve Me now and let us no longer have any lapses in service. Remain with me, your heavenly Father, who seeks to direct all that has an impact on you. I will bring every event in your life and turn it into something that benefits your soul and gives you eternal satisfaction and joy. But not all in my life is good, you are thinking. I know that, My child. That is why you need Me. I can turn the pain, the anguish, the mistakes and grief, into strength, wisdom, patience, and joy. Truly, if you are detached from the world and from worldly things, you can experience a foretaste of heaven on earth and then you will have less desire for earthly things. You will have a clearer, more defined focus. You will have less difficulty with the idea of leaving the earth and making the journey to your home in heaven. Believe Me when I tell you that everything I say, all that I share with you, I share with you for your own benefit. I am your Father and a Father sees to the needs of His children. Use Me, children to calm your spirit and direct your path. It is for this reason that I come to you now.

God the Father

as given to Anne, a lay apostle

No growth is possible in confusion.

To relax mind and body at frequent intervals will also aid remarkably but the most important of all is the attainment of the consciousness of peace.

There is a state within us where all is still… To cultivate the consciousness of this state is the real secret of attaining a permanent mental state of peace.

We always become in the without as we feel in the within.

Become more conscious of the calm that is within you and your personality will become more calm.

Christian Larson

Successful people are solution oriented.

Successful people respond effectively to problems and look for the good in every situation. When you have clear goals, written and rewritten, visualized and emotionalized, you trigger your conscious, subconscious, and superconscious minds into generating a continuous flow of ideas for goal attainment.

Brian Tracy

The same stillness that you feel within yourself when in the consciousness of peace, will unfold itself through your entire system and you will become peaceful in every part of mind and body.

## Peace and Poise

Peace is a restful attitude while Poise is a working attitude. In Peace you feel absolutely still. In Poise you feel and hold the mighty power within you ready for action. The poised mind combines calmness with power.

The art of being peaceful and powerful at the same time is an art that has received little attention; but it is something that is extremely important and no one who desires to learn to think and act for results can afford to neglect this high art for a moment.

Think according to the laws of growth.

Think for a definite purpose.

This is the principle upon which to act when thinking for results, and whoever resolves to think in this manner only will soon find remarkable changes for the better taking place in every department of his life.

Christian Larson

*On The Bright Side*

## Do Something Every Day

You will always be compensated in life in direct proportion to the value of your contribution. If you want to get more out, you have to put more in.

Go the extra mile.

Get up a little earlier.

Work a little harder.

Stay a little longer.

Your success in life will be in direct proportion to what you do after you do what you are expected to do.

Brian Tracy

Every one of us is the sum total of his own thoughts.

Earl Nightingale

I worked for a menial's hire,

Only to learn, dismayed,

That any wages I had asked of life,

Life would have willingly paid.

Jessie B. Rittenhouse

Mind is the Master-power that moulds and makes,

And Man is Mind, and evermore he takes

The tool of thought and shaping what he wills,

Brings forth a thousand joys, a thousand ills:

He thinks in secret, and it comes to pass:

Environment is but his looking glass.

James Allen

Before you can change the course of your destiny, you must first gain access to that secret place within yourself where your own future is being created moment by moment by moment. Yes, there is such a location. It's Real. And yes, you can learn to dwell there and direct your destiny.

This truly timeless place, where all of your life-choices are made for you, is what we understand, in concept, as the Present Moment. But this state of True Now is not just an idea. It's a place of extraordinary and measureless power, for the True Present Moment is actually a Cosmic Seed of a sort, from out of which springs all that comes later.

In any and every given moment of your life, you are either in command of yourself…or you are being commanded.

Guy Finley

Determine never to be idle. No person will have occasion to complain of the want of time, who never loses any.

It is wonderful how much may be done, if we are always doing.

Thomas Jefferson

Time will pass anyway:

Get going, keep going

Earl Nightingale

Momentum Principle of Success

It takes considerable energy to get yourself into motion and moving. But it takes much less energy to keep yourself moving, once you get going.

Brian Tracy

You can learn how to be that rarest of individuals who is always going exactly where he or she wants to be going; one whose entire life experience – each and every step along the chosen way – never fails to be self-enriching. This is the life that's intended to be your destiny!

Guy Finley

My servants often have difficulty overcoming their self-will. Brothers and sisters, self-will does not lead to Me. Self-will leads away from Me. That concept is very simple. You may hear souls saying, "What is His will? Help me to know His will." Well, truly, if I am asked, I will answer. Your Jesus, who calls you so firmly into service right now, will not leave you wondering. Be certain you are asking Me to show you My will in the silence of contemplation. There are times when souls know My will but find it repugnant. You must know that I understand this revulsion for the self-sacrificing that often accompanies My will. But children of the all-powerful God, know that this offering of your will can make you a saint quite quickly. I did not want to suffer great torture and pain in My body. Believe Me when I say that I shuddered in contemplation of the cross. Yet, the cross was the Father's will for Me. So be it. I shouldered My cross in humility and obedience and through the cross I redeemed you. You are worth the sacrifice. And it was temporary. The sacrifices you are being asked to make are also temporary. You are not and will not be asked to relinquish anything for eternity. Your eternity, based on the beautiful merits of your sacrifices and service, will be filled with joy and reward. So you, like Me, are being asked to carry this cross or that cross, make this sacrifice or that sacrifice, for a short time, so that I, through your obedience and cooperation, can bring other souls to heaven.

Consider how important each soul is to Me. Consider Me, Jesus, in the form of My humanity. As I suffered anguish in the Garden, I was tempted with every form of temptation. Let us say that the enemy offered Me every soul on earth, but one. For stepping away from the chance of saving this one soul, I could escape the cross. Add to the consideration that this one soul might reject Me and be lost anyway. Would I be tempted? Would you?

Now consider that this one soul was yours.

What do you think I would say?

I assure you, My beloved, I said NO.

Do not hold back from Me, little servants. Do not sidestep the divine will. Your family needs you and I need you.

Jesus

as given to Anne, a lay apostle

*On The Bright Side*

Persist until you succeed.

Self- Discipline is the core quality.

Persistence is Self-Discipline in action.

Brian Tracy

Imagineering: The use of mental images to build factual results.

Form an image. What you image may ultimately become a fact if held mentally with self-sufficient faith.

God is now filling my mind with courage, with peace, with calm assurance. God is now guiding me to the right decisions.

Faith can always overcome fear.

That which I have greatly believed has come upon me.

Norman Vincent Peale

*On The Bright Side*

The only thing we have to fear is fear itself.

Franklin D Roosevelt


Be not afraid. I go before you always. Come follow Me and I will give you rest.

John M. Talbot


Never give in. Never give in. Never, never, never, never – in nothing, great or small, large or petty – never give in, except to convictions of honour and good sense. Never yield to force. Never yield to the apparently overwhelming might of the enemy.

Winston Churchill


Our doubts are traitors and make us lose the good we oft might win by fearing to attempt.

William Shakespeare


Thought is a magnet; and the longed for pleasure or boon or aim or object is the steel; and its attainment hangs but on the measure of what thy soul can feel.

Ella Wilcox

*On The Bright Side*

Adversity has the effect of drawing out strength and qualities of a man that would have lain dormant in its absence.

Herodotus

The meaning of life is to find your gift.

The purpose of life is to give it away.

William Shakespeare

I want to speak to those mothers who have lost children through sickness or tragedy. Dearest mother, whose heart is broken, you will see your child again, and when you do you will see that your child has been joyful and cared for in your brief separation. Do not grieve if you can help it, but spread joy to those who also grieve. Ask me and I will help you to do this because I know that it seems an impossible thing. All is well in Heaven. Have no fear that your child is not with God. We must all cooperate with Heaven during this time, so prayerfully consider what it is that Jesus needs from you.

Mary, an unknown saint

as given to Anne, a lay apostle

Endurance and perseverance is what make them great.


Persistence guarantees your goal.


Persistence and Determination

Get to it – Stick to it.

Brian Tracy


Our greatest glory is not in never falling but in rising every time we fall.

Confucius


There is not failure except in no longer trying. There is no defeat, except from within, no really insurmountable barrier save our own inherent weakness of purpose.

Elbert Hubbard


People are always blaming their circumstances for what they are.

I don't believe in circumstances. The people who get on in this world are the people who get up and look for the circumstances they want and if they can't find them, they make them.

George Bernard Shaw

Imagine yourself successful.

Visualize the person you desire to become.

Reflect on your past successes. Every success, large or small is proof that you are capable of achieving more success.

Set Definite Goals- Have a clear direction of where you want to go. Take immediate corrective action if you deviate.

Respond positively to life;

positive self-image;

your decisions are within your control.

Napoleon Hill

The knowledge of our Power

The courage to Dare

The Faith to Do

How is wisdom secured?

By concentration; it is an unfoldment; it comes from within.

Charles Haanel

Habit is a cable;

We weave a thread of it every day,

And at last

We cannot break it.

Horace Mann

Faith is the eternal elixir which gives life, power, and action to the impulse of thought.

Napoleon Hill

For each time you have the awareness not to choose from that bank of old patterns produced by your limited thought nature, new and higher alternatives appear before your inner eyes.

Guy Finley

If you think in negative terms, you get negative results.

If you think in positive terms, you will achieve positive results.

Believe and Succeed

Norman Vincent Peale

What the mind profoundly expects it tends to receive.

If with all your heart (that is the secret) you reach out creatively towards your heart's desire, your reach will not be in vain.

Faith Power works wonders.

Norman Vincent Peale

I can do all things through Christ which strengtheneth me.

Philippians 4:13

I believe God gives me the power to attain what I really want. I expect the best and with God's help will attain the best.

A man who is self-reliant, positive, optimistic, and undertakes his work with the assurance of success magnetizes his condition. He draws to himself the creative powers of the universe.

Take the best into your mind and only that. Nurture it, concentrate on it, emphasize it, visualize it, prayerize it, surround it with faith.

Make it your obsession. Expect the best and spiritually creative mind-power aided by God-power will produce the best.

Norman Vincent Peale

If you **think** you are beaten, you are.

If you **think** you dare not, you don't.

If you like to win, but you **think** you can't.

It's almost certain you won't.


If you **think** you'll lose, you're lost.

For out of the world we find,

Success begins with a person's will –

It's all in the **state of mind**


If you **think** you are outclassed, you are.

You've got to **think high** to rise.

You've got to be sure of yourself before

You can ever win a prize.


Life's battles don't always go

To the stronger or faster man.

But sooner or later the one who wins

Is the one **Who Thinks He Can!**

Walter D. Wintle

Be definite in everything you do and never leave unfinished thoughts in the mind. Form the habit of reaching definite decisions on all subjects.

Remember that your dominating thoughts attract through a definite law of nature, by the shortest and most convenient route, their physical counterpart. Be careful what your thoughts dwell upon.

One's dominating desires can be crystallized into their physical equivalents through definiteness of purpose backed by definiteness of plans, with the aid of nature's law of hypnotic rhythm and time!

Napoleon Hill

Do today what others won't

So tomorrow you will have what others don't.

Robert Montgomery paraphrasing unknown author

You are the greatest miracle in the world.

The laws of Happiness and Success are 4:

1) Count your blessings    (Gratitude)

2) Proclaim your rarity    (Realize your uniqueness)

3) Go another mile    (Be persistent)

4) Use wisely your Power of Choice    (Use your Free Will wisely)

Do all things with Love.

Love for yourself

Love for others

Love for God

You are capable of great wonders.

Your potential is unlimited.

Never demean yourself again!

Never settle for the crumbs of life!

Never hide your talents from this day hence!

Og Mandino

## 10 Rules for Success

1) Do your own thinking on all occasions.

2) Decide definitely what you want from life; then create a plan for attaining it and be willing to sacrifice.

3) Analyze temporary defeat and extract from it the seed of an equivalent advantage.

4) Be willing to render useful service equivalent to the value of all material things you demand of life, and render the service first.

5) Recognize that your brain is a receiving set that can be attuned to receive communications from God to help you transmute your desires into their physical equivalent.

6) Recognize that your greatest asset is time, the only thing except the power of thought which you own outright, and the one thing which can be shaped into whatever material things you want. Budget your time so none of it is wasted.

7) Recognize the truth, that fear generally is a filler with which the devil occupies the unused portion of your mind. It is only a state of mind which you can control.

8) Pray and have faith that you will receive what you pray for.

9) Never accept from life what you don't want.

10) Remember that your dominating thoughts attract. Be careful what your thoughts dwell on.

Definiteness of purpose

Mastery over self

Learning from adversity

Thinking through your plan before you act.

Napoleon Hill

Your Power of Choice

Choose to love….rather than hate

Choose to laugh….rather than cry

Choose to create….rather than destroy

Choose to persevere….rather than quit

Choose to praise….rather than gossip

Choose to heal….rather than wound

Choose to give….rather than steal

Choose to act…rather than procrastinate

Choose to grow….rather than rot

Choose to pray….rather than curse

Choose to live….rather than die

The choice is exclusively yours.


Remember then, the four laws of happiness and success:

Count your blessings.

Proclaim your rarity.

Go another mile.

Use wisely your power of choice.

And, one more to fulfill the other four. Do all things with love…love for yourself, love for all others, and love for Me.

You are the greatest miracle in the world.

Og Mandino

Little servants, seek only the divine will. On each day I want you to consider what I require from you. This means you will often find yourself realigning your activities to fit into My needs. Your time must be fruitful for the Kingdom and for that to occur, you must always ask Me what I would like you to do with your time. You see that I wish there to be constant communication between us. This may seem like a burden to you at first, but you will quickly become comfortable with unity to heaven. If heaven is to flow through you into the world, and that is the goal, you must let heaven direct everything. You know that we in heaven are willing to do that for you. We know that you are striving to allow heaven to direct you. So all that is needed is practice. How often we have asked you to practice. You are coming along, little apostles, and you are witnessing the way it is to be, with you serving and Me directing. Move forward daily, always forward, in My service, and you will see souls returning. I am with you in everything.

Jesus

as given to Anne, a lay apostle

The drip, drip of a drop of water,

Over and over, can carve through rock but

The rush of a torrent of water

Passes without leaving a trace.


Perseverance

Repetition

Love

Goals

Work/Action

Bit by bit


I am in charge of my life.

I am responsible for the outcome.

Be Positive – Be filled with gratitude

Goals – daily, weekly, monthly, yearly, Lifetime

Enthusiastic

Know that you are unique (no one is like you anywhere)

Know you are loved

Choose to be positive

Choose to feel Gratitude

Choose your goals

Take action on your goals

Be enthusiastic

You are unique, you are loved, you have a job to do that only you can do.

Enjoy this day today…

And tomorrow, tomorrow.

Choose Success and Happiness. The choice is yours

Og Mandino

We must speak today to all mothers who are alone in the parenting of their children. Dear mother you are supposed to have help, it is true. It is very difficult to be alone in a job that requires two people. Do not be afraid, though, because in this situation Heaven steps in with great power. You must tell yourself to be brave. You will never be alone in any problem that involves your parenting. God is the Father of your children and He has placed them in your care. He will see that you have everything you need to shepherd your children through their childhoods. You must communicate with Him constantly about your fears, your concerns over their development and, of course, providing for their material needs. You should also confide in Mary, the Blessed Mother. She was a constant source of comfort and support to me in my own parenting. Between Jesus and Mary, you will have all of the assistance you require. Please believe that if you are following the path to Heaven, your children will also follow the path to Heaven. A great deal of the work of parenting is done in the example that you set. If you walk constantly toward Christ, your children will recognize that path, and they will recognize when they have left that path. You are not a single parent, dear mother, because you are part of a heavenly team that is going to see that your children receive exactly what they need to serve Christ. You have many friends in Heaven who understand your struggles. Cry out to them when you are worried. When you experience joy and there is nobody there to share it with you, share it with Jesus. He will experience such delight if you do this. Our Jesus wants people to rely on Him in grief, of course, but He takes special joy in a soul calling Him in to share family happiness or accomplishment. This will create for Jesus a firm role in your family and He will not disappoint you or fail to pull His share of the weight. Such a thing is not possible. You must always remember this, dear little mother who feels so afraid at times. You are not alone. Speak constantly to Heaven about your children. Heaven is filled with souls who cherish them as much as you do. Mothers, there will be children who divert from the heavenly path at times. You must try not to be alarmed because this is not uncommon. Pray constantly for these souls, of course, but show them peace in the face of their rebellion. Explain that they have left the heavenly path and that if they are off the path when Christ comes, there is the danger of not getting back to the path in time to get to Heaven. I speak of course about older children who have rejected Christ and Christian living. I hear the cries of mothers who worry over these rebellious ones. That is why I speak of it. Remember that Christ is all mercy to a mother. Your maternal prayers are powerful so continue to pray for your child, but do not think that all is lost, regardless of the circumstances. Even in the direst cases, Jesus will forgive all for the sake of a holy mother. So really, there is nothing you should upset yourself with, dear mothers. Our Lord will save your children and protect their eternities. Your job is to cooperate with Him. Speak the truth to your children fearlessly, in kindness and love, and they will belong to Christ.

Mary, an unknown saint

as given to Anne, a lay apostle

*On The Bright Side*

People with goals succeed because they know where they are going.

Earl Nightingale

A man's life is what his thoughts make of it.

Marcus Aurelius

Human beings can alter their life by altering their attitudes of mind.

If you only care enough for a result, you will almost certainly ascertain it.

William James

If thou canst believe, all things are possible to him that believeth.

Mark 9:23

Thoughts are things. Thought is a force, a vibration.

Like attracts like in the thought world.

The cause of success is in the individual.

William W. Atkinson


It is mathematically certain that you can succeed if you will find out the cause of success, and develop it to sufficient strength, and apply it properly to your work; for the application of a sufficient cause cannot fail to produce a given effect.

Orson Swett Marden


The most valuable thing that ever comes into a life is that experience, that book, that sermon, that person, that incident, that emergency, that accident that catastrophe – that *something* which touches the springs of a man's inner nature and flings open the doors of his great within revealing its hidden resources.

Quoted by Orson S. Marden


To become <u>convinced</u> that you can succeed is the first requisite to success.

Wallace D. Wattles


The something in men who succeed is called Active Power Consciousness. Power Consciousness is what you feel when you know that you <u>can</u> do a thing; and you know <u>how</u> to do a thing. If you know you can do a thing and know how to do it, it is impossible that you should fail to do it if you really try.

Charles Haanel

It is I, the Father of All, who speaks to this small soul. I wish to give My children both notice and direction. If you are following Me, continue to follow Me, but in a more dedicated fashion. Ask yourself on this day, "What can I do for My Father in heaven?" I will put the answer in your heart, little souls, and you will have My request. Then you must step out in faith and complete the task I have asked of you. Through this first step, you will discover how I am going to work through you. Ask Me for direction, and in an enhanced way, you will be directed…

God the Father

as given to Anne, a lay apostle

Your only way of reaching a better environment is by making constructive use of your present environment. Only the complete use of your present environment will place you in a more desirable one.

Orson S. Marden

When you are in full Power-Consciousness, you will approach the task in an absolutely successful frame of mind. Every thought will be a successful thought, every action a successful action; and if every thought and action is successful, the sum total of all your actions cannot be failure.

Wallace Wattles

Every day and night, think of your subconscious mind, try to feel it, you will soon be able to become conscious of it. Hold this consciousness and say with deep earnest feeling; I CAN SUCCEED! All that is possible to anyone is possible to me, I AM Successful. I Do succeed, for I am full of the Power of Success.

Wallace D. Wattles

It is within your power to make a greater success in your business than anyone has ever made before you.

Wallace D. Wattles

If you wish to extend your present business remember that you can only do it by doing in the most perfect manner the business you already have. When you put life enough into your business to more than fill it, the surplus will get you more business. Do not reach out after more until you have life to spare after doing perfectly all that you have to do now. And remember, it is the perfection with which you do what you have to do now that extends your field and brings you in touch with a larger environment.

You can get what you want only by ACTING.

Consider that you can act only in your present environment;

and do not try to act now upon environment of the future.

Also, remember that your actions will not have dynamic moving power unless you have an unwavering faith that you get what you want.

To get more, you must make constructive use of what you have. You must do perfectly all that you can do now; and it is the law that by doing perfectly all that you can do now you will become able to do later things which you cannot do now.

The doing to perfection of one thing invariably provides us with the equipment for doing the next larger thing because it is a principle inherent in nature that life continuously advances. Every person who does one thing perfect, is instantly presented with the opportunity to begin doing the next larger thing, because it is a principle inherent in nature that life continuously advances.

Wallace D. Wattles

Form a clear mental picture of what you want; hold the purpose to get it; do everything perfectly, not in a servile spirit, but because you are a master mind; keep unwavering faith in your ultimate attainment of your goal and you cannot fail to move forward.

To make the at-one-ment, you must see that your business gives to all who deal with you a full equivalent in life for the money value of what you take from them. I say in life; that does not necessarily mean in money value.

What you seek for yourself you seek for all.

Wallace D. Wattles

What things so ever ye desire when ye pray,

believe that ye receive them, and you shall have them.

Mark 11:24

Every one of us is the sum total of his own thoughts. He is where he is because that is exactly where he really wants to be, whether he'll admit that or not. Each of us must live off the fruits of his thoughts in the future because what you think today and tomorrow, next month or next year, will mold your life and determine your future. You're guided by your mind.

To be successful, we must be willing to pay the price. Now, what is that price? Well, it's many things. First, it's understanding that we literally become what we think about – we must control our thoughts if we are to control our lives. It's understanding fully that as you sow, so shall you reap.

Secondly, it's cutting away all the fetters from the mind and permitting it to soar as it was Divinely designed to do. It's the realization that your limitations are self-imposed and that the opportunities for you today are enormous beyond belief. It's rising above narrow-minded pettiness and prejudice.

Thirdly, to use all your courage to force yourself to think positively on your own problem.

- to set a definite and clearly defined goal for yourself
- to let your marvelous mind think about your goals from all possible angles
- to let your imagination speculate freely upon many different possible solutions
- to refuse to believe there are any circumstances sufficiently strong to defeat you in the accomplishment of your purpose
- to act promptly and decisively when your course is clear and to keep constantly aware of the fact that you are, at this moment, standing in the middle of your acres of diamonds.

Fourth, to save at least 10% of what you earn.

Earl Nightingale

*On The Bright Side*

1) You will become what you think about.

2) Remember the word <u>imagination</u>. Let your mind soar.

3) <u>Courage</u> – concentrate on your goal every day.

4) Save 10% of what you earn, and ACTION. Ideas are worth less unless you <u>act</u> on <u>them</u>.

Earl Nightingale

The greatest achievement was at first and for a time a dream. The oak sleeps in an acorn; the bird waits in the egg; and in the highest vision of the soul a waking angel stirs. Dreams are the Seedlings of Reality.

James Allen

Do – Then Believe

Believe – Then Achieve

I feel like succeeding today!

A burning desire to be and to do is the starting point from which the dreamer must take off. Dreams are not born of indifference, laziness, or lack of ambition.

Our only limitations are those we set up in our own minds.

You will become as small as your controlling desire; as great as your dominant aspiration.

In all human affairs there are efforts, and there are results, and the strength of the effort is the measure of the result. Chance is not. "Gifts," power, material, intellectual, and spiritual possessions are the fruits of effort; they are thoughts completed, objects accomplished, visions realized.

The vision that you glorify in your mind, the Ideal that you enthrone in your heart – this you will build your life by, this you will become.

James Allen

My children of light, how filled with joy I will be when I welcome you home to your reward. It is always My will that you return to Me. Children, you will be struck by how comfortable you feel in heaven. You will feel as though you are in your true home for the first time. Once you follow Me and become My servant, you have an advanced awareness that the earth holds no true home for you. My servants must be prepared to serve in whatever place I call them. They must serve whatever people I require them to serve. My servants may be called at any time to do whatever the Kingdom requires. This is the way it is in a family. You are in My family. As members of the heavenly family, you are to be interested in the welfare of the other members, your brothers and sisters. Children of the light, consider each and every soul on this earth your brother and sister. Your concern should be how to bring each soul on earth home to heaven with you. "This is far too big, Father," you say. Well, dear little one, that is My goal. And because it is my My goal, it must be your goal. A good child, an obedient child, always looks out for the interests of his Father, And that is what My servants must do. Now instead of finding this a frightening, overwhelming task, I want you to say, "This task will be an easy thing, because My Father will do all of the work. All I need do is rise each day with a spirit of willingness. If I do that, My Father, along with His Son, and the Holy Spirit, and all of the inhabitants of heaven will work through me in a miraculous way and souls will be saved." A word here, a smile there, a kindness there, an act of humility when pride would be tempting, these small acts bring souls back to the family and I can then bring then to heaven. My dearest little ones, your Father is calling out to you in hope and in love. Hear My voice on this day, this day when mercy is being extended to your world. The sacrifices of many of your brothers and sisters are what obtained this day of mercy when only justice was called for. I your heavenly Creator, wish you to make the fullest possible use of this time of grace. Join Me now, join the saints, join the souls of the just on earth, and together all united, we will bring the souls of many back to My heart before the time of upheaval.

God the Father

as given to Anne, a lay apostle

My little ones feel great joy in communicating with Me. That is the smallest foretaste of heaven. In heaven, you will have instant and constant communication with Me. We will take such joy in each other, dear children. There is a complete absence of want in heaven. You will search in vain for the poor, the troubled, and the sick. Everywhere you look you will view another tableau of peace and serenity. Souls will seek knowledge and find it. Souls will seek wisdom and obtain it. Souls will seek understanding from others and others will instantly understand them. Such sympathetic listening will take place in heaven, My children. You will know nothing of anxiety for loved ones in heaven because all will be well and all will be decided. There will be no uncertainty in the hearts of My children. Dear ones, this is your destiny. This is your inheritance for which you were created. Your time on earth is a small capsule of time designed to give you the opportunity to obtain your place in heaven. Use the gifts I have given you and you will find no limit to what you can achieve on earth. All heavenly help is available. "But we cannot see it," reply My children in their poor little hearts. Dear children, as you have been told, you cannot see the wind, but you see the power of the wind and you see the beautiful things that can be achieved when you harness that power. I am the same. How does one harness God? Simply by praying. As you are My servants, I am also your servant, in the sense that a father wants all for his children and gives all to his children. If a child continually refuses a gift from his father, the father knows to stop forcing the gift on that child. The wise father knows that the child cannot be given the gift until the child is ready to see the value of the gift and accept it. This may not be the father's wish. The father wishes to give the child every gift available and every gift that is valuable to that child. But the wise father waits for the opportunity to direct the child and that opportunity comes when the child begins to listen. Listen to Me, children. I have many graces to give you that you require for your salvation. How sad for Me that My graces are refused and rejected as though they are worthless. I created your world for your pleasure and edification. I did not create your world so that you could sin against each other and sin against Me. Look carefully into your life now. Say to Me, "God, my Father, help me to understand." I will not refuse this prayer, dearest child destined to be held against My heart. I will not refuse you. I will help you to understand exactly what keeps you from Me. And together, with all of the assistance of heaven, we will bring you to your rightful place. My courage is boundless and I give you a share of that courage. The world will pass away, dear ones, but you will be with Me

God the Father

as given to Anne, a lay apostle

*On The Bright Side*

Our financial return will be in direct proportion to our service to others.

Earl Nightingale

But he that is greatest among you shall be your servant.

Matthew 23:11

Ask and it shall be given you.

Seek and ye shall find.

Knock and it shall be opened unto you.

For everyone that asketh, receiveth.

And he that seeketh, findeth.

And to him that knocketh, it shall be opened.

Matthew 7:7

Thought cannot conceive of anything that may not be brought into expression.
He who first uttered it may be only the suggester, but the doer will appear.

Wilson

Develop concentration

*On The Bright Side*

The only way to keep from going backward is to keep going forward.

Charles Haanel

Eternal vigilance is the price of success.

Quoted by Charles Haanel

There are three steps and each one is absolutely essential.

You must first have the knowledge of your power;

Second, the courage to dare;

Third, the faith to do.

The intention governs the attention.

Charles Haanel

Happy Moments…..Praise God

Difficult Moments…..Seek God

Quiet Moments…..Worship God

Painful Moments…..Trust God

Every Moment…..Thank God

Rick Warren

*On The Bright Side*

My children, as your Father, I retain a certain amount of authority over you. It is good when you acknowledge this and bow before Me. I do not want souls to bow before Me because they have been forced. I prefer My children to serve Me from motives of love and loyalty. Loyalty to God is something that has fallen by the wayside in your world. I gaze upon My creatures, looking for faces that look up to Me in love, and I find so few in this time. Many of you have been caught up in the noise of your current world. I do not speak of the natural noise of wind through trees, water from streams, lakes, and oceans, and the noises of animals as they serve their God in all their busyness. I speak of the artificial noise that you surround yourself with, in an effort to feel safe. Sit in silence, please. Remove this clamor from your life. I say this with all authority and understanding of the needs of the creatures I have created. Your spirits suffocate under the attack of all this noise. In silence comes peace, the peace within which I would speak to you. Dearest little ones, destined for heaven you will not know how to conduct yourselves in the next world with its beautiful quiet. There will be sounds in heaven, but beautiful, organized sounds destined to bring joy to the spirits of My little ones. How you will weep for joy at the sound of the angels as they combine their voices to praise Me and entertain the saints. And you will all be saints, dear ones, if you listen to My voice within you. There are also the beautiful sounds of My creation. Children, if there is a sound that gives you joy, you will experience it in heaven in the most profound way that you can imagine. Indeed, you cannot imagine it, but you can dream about it and every so often I will give you a sample of heavenly sound in your life. Watch for these little experiences, children. You will find them on your earth. Because of your limited vision, which is My will for you at this time, you cannot experience heaven in its fullness. But your God often visits you with a portion of your inheritance. When you experience these things, look to Me in joy and, truly you will find Me looking back at you in all love and tenderness, Thank Me for these gifts. They are intended to encourage you. Children, close your eyes for a moment. Open them. That is how quickly it will seem to you that you and I will meet. Your life is but a blink in time compared to eternity. Will you not give Me the smallest bit of credit? Look up to Me now and tell Me you love Me. Perhaps you are uncomfortable because you do not feel you know Me. I want you to remember that I know you. I have always known you because I created you. I chose to send you to earth now. I had reasons for My choice of your birth time and those reasons still exist. So serve, little one. Serve. I will reveal Myself to you if you invite Me. Tell Me you would like to know Me better. I will not refuse such a request. You will become My intimate friend if you make such a prayer to Me with your heart. Even if you have the smallest interest in knowing Me, I will come to you. I love you. I see your soul in all its future beauty. You cannot imagine what you are capable of doing for the heavenly Kingdom if you will allow Me to work through you. In this time of peace, allow Me to put My love in your soul. You will not regret coming to know Me. Such a thing is not possible. You will only thank Me for coming to you. So do not delay, little child. Come to your Father, who wants only your happiness and welfare.

God the Father

as given to Anne, a lay apostle

Success is the progressive realization of a worthy ideal. If a man is working towards a predetermined goal and knows where he is going, that man is a success. If he's not doing that, he's a failure.

Success is the progressive realization of a worthy ideal.

Keep calm and cheerful.
Don't let petty things annoy you.

Earl Nightingale

The opposite of courage in our society is not cowardness, it is conformity.

Rollo May

Imagination is the beginning of creation. You imagine what you desire, you will what you imagine and at last you create what you will.

George Bernard Shaw

I am joyful to be talking to my little ones about angels because I know that the thought of angels makes you happy. So often in these times we are discussing difficult matters, so it is a relief for me to talk to you about something that is lovely and good. Children, your Jesus has asked that you walk in peace. He needs this from you, as His plan cannot be realized unless you cooperate with that request. Only through each one of you will peace flow into your troubled world. So, because this is so important, I am going to make a suggestion. Whenever you are troubled, and feel your peace has fled, you must speak to your angel guardian. Ask your little heavenly soldier to hasten to your assistance and obtain the graces you need to recover your peace. This is the perfect request from you because there is nothing heaven likes better than to help a soul in the world be at peace. You see, we know how important it is and you might say that these graces are easily obtained when the request comes from you. So say this when you are losing your spiritual balance and your peace, "Dearest angel guardian, I desire to serve Jesus by remaining at peace. Please obtain for me the graces necessary to maintain His divine peace in my heart." You will not be disappointed, little ones. The graces will come to you.

Blessed Mother

as given to Anne, a lay apostle

*On The Bright Side*

I will make this day worthwhile.

That marvelous future which you have dreamed of so long will be exactly what you put into your todays.

It is so much easier to dream of a great big success tomorrow than to try to make today a big success.

A negative mind is fatal to success.

A positive mind is sure to succeed.

Change your thoughts and you change your world.

Norman Vincent Peale

Seize the Day!

C = E / R     Current = Voltage / Resistance

Current – The energy we use to accomplish anything of worth. Power output needs energy to perform.

Voltage – This is the source – it is all around us – it comes from and is God. This is a constant. The voltage doesn't change. Everyone has access to the same amount.

Resistance – This is something that interferes with the amount of voltage that can be transferred or utilized. If resistance is high then it will lower the actual output of energy. Some forms of resistance are: fear; negative thoughts; hate; doubts; trauma; low self-esteem.

Resistance is the variable. This is what is different in individuals. This is what we have to work on to attain great heights and achieve what we are here to achieve. We all have access to God (Voltage-Source). But each individual has his own set of variables that are supplying resistance which will lesson the final accomplishments.

If we want more energy to go into the final output we must lower the resistance. This means we must learn to think positively, get over fears, self-doubts, past traumas, disappointments. When we eliminate our resistance qualities our creative output will soar. Our accomplishments will multiply. We are all capable of so much more but we hold ourselves back by not eliminating the resistance.

There is a beauty in mathematics that can only come from God. An underlying simplicity in something that is seemingly so complicated.

C = E / R. That is all you need to know to succeed. That is the simple part. Now the complicated part; what do you want? And what is holding you back? The majority of people never really answer this question in their life-times. If you do know what you want, why don't you have it? What is holding you back? That's the complicated part. Where is your resistance coming from? Fear? Hate? Trauma? Low self-image? Negative thoughts?

Your resistance has to be identified, faced, and resolved. Then your accomplishments will soar.

When you want to accomplish something, say you are doing it – Desire must come first – see yourself doing it - visualize every detail – feel it, use it, start on the path towards it. Use what you have now, where you are now, but turn your face towards where you want to go (not where you don't want to go).Take time every day to revisit where you are going. What steps are you taking today to get there?

With too much resistance no current is delivered – no matter how much is available.

C (creative output) changes in direct proportion to R (resistance). E (Source from God) is a constant it never changes or diminishes. What changes is the amount of the resistance. Lower the resistance and you raise the output.

Fear is the greatest form of resistance. Fear of failure, fear of not being good enough, fear of lack, fear of pain, fear of unacceptance, fear of being laughed at, fear of not being loved.

All forms of resistance lesson the power we can pull from the Infinite Source of power – God. God permeates and penetrates everything around us.

The antenna that draws the power towards us is desire. First you must want something or have the desire for attainment.

*Based on writings from Jose Silva*

Every thought therefore is a cause and every condition an effect. For this reason it is absolutely essential that you control your thoughts so as to bring forth only desirable conditions.

The world within is the cause, the world without the effect; to change the effect, you must change the cause.

You cannot entertain weak, harmful negative thoughts ten hours a day and expect to bring about beautiful, strong and harmonious conditions by ten minutes of strong positive creative thought.

Thought is energy. Active thought is active energy; concentrated thought is a concentrated energy. Thought concentrated on a definite purpose becomes power.

Thought forms the mold or matrix from which the substance expresses.

Charles Haanel

*On The Bright Side*

The personal man is the direct, or indirect, result of subconscious thought; subconscious thought is determined by mental attitudes; and man can enter into any mental attitude desired; therefore, any change, modification or condition decided upon may be produced in the personality.

In the last analysis, subconscious thought is the fundamental cause of everything that exists or transpires in the personal nature of man; and as man may subconsciously think whatever he desires to think, the nature, the life, and the destiny of his personality are in his own hands.

Christian Larson

A success is anyone who is doing a predetermined job because that's what he decided to do deliberately.

Instead of competing all we have to do is create.

Earl Nightingale

Obstacles are those frightening things you see when you take your eyes off the target.

Henry James

My children, how often I have looked upon you, surrounded by God's angels but feeling so alone. These angels have soft little hearts and they grieve with you when you are sad. So often they seek to comfort you with heavenly thoughts but you do not accept these ideas. Allow these beautiful thoughts into your hearts and you will feel the consolation with which the angels seek to bless you. Again I say, and I understand that I am repeating myself, you must spend time in silence so that we can place these lovely thoughts in your hearts. You understand that communicating with heaven is not like communicating with earth. We do not shout, usually, and you must listen with your soul. In days past, there was not this constant noise. Children, think about why the enemy never leaves you in peace. It is like a child's attempt to distract someone so that bad news cannot be communicated about him. When you feel distracted, and feel your peace is slipping from you, ask yourself how much time during that particular day you spent in silence, contemplating God. I am certain that it was not enough. So find silence. Seek it out. Value it. Understand that this is not wasted time, but the most important time of your day.

Blessed Mother

as given to Anne, a lay apostle

Harmony in the world within means the ability to control our thoughts,
and to determine for ourselves how any experience is to affect us.

Harmony in the world within results in optimism and affluence;

affluence within results in affluence without.

The secret of all power, all achievement and all possessions depends
upon our method of thinking.

We must "be" before we can "do" and

we can "do" only to the extent which we "are" and

what we "are" depends upon what we think.

Charles Haanel

Keep your mind fixed on what you want in life,

not on what you don't want.

Get into action.

Napoleon Hill

My children of the world, look for Me. Look for the signs in your world that I am present. Some would have you believe that I am no longer actively directing the outcome of this time. Children, can you believe that I am no longer actively directing the outcome of this time. Children, can you believe that I would lovingly lead My children for centuries, since the beginning of the world, and then leave? Would I really turn away from My precious creatures? This idea is fooling many souls today. They proceed in their lives as though I do not exist and as though there will be no reckoning for decisions against Me, against others, and at times even against nature, as I created nature. I see all. I will judge every action. I will reward every decision made by one soul for the benefit of another. In the same way, I will challenge every decision made by one soul to the detriment of another. Children, all is being recorded. You will account for your life. I am merciful. I am merciful to a degree that will astound you. But you must allow Me to be merciful. You must accept My mercy. You cannot scorn My mercy, child. Allow Me to exercise My mercy in your life. "How must we do that, Father?" you ask. I will tell you. You must say this to Me: "God my Father in heaven, You are all mercy. You love me and see my every sin. God, I call on You now as the merciful Father. Forgive my every sin. Wash away the stains on my soul so that I may once again rest in complete innocence. I trust You, Father in heaven. I rely on You. I thank You. Amen."

I am acting as the merciful Father in these days, children. Pray this prayer to Me and I will respond in mercy. Your soul will be washed clean. Little children of My Church on earth, you must not neglect the sacraments. Experience the sacramental graces of the confessional, and say this prayer. In this way the residue of sin will be removed from your souls painlessly. Trust My words, children. Do as your Father says. The wise one understands that a Father acts only in the best interest of His children. And so I act at this time.

God the Father

as given to Anne, a lay apostle

Stop trying to get something for nothing. There is no such thing as a free lunch. You must give to receive. You must give mental attention to your goals, ideals, and enterprises, and your deeper mind will back you up.

Specialize in your particular field and try to know more about it than anyone else.

Find out what you love to do and do it. If you don't know your true expression, ask for guidance, and the lead will come.

Joseph Murphy

Take nothing from anybody without giving a full equivalent in life; the more you give, the better for you.

Wallace Wattles

I want to speak directly to souls at this time. Many souls are crying out for Me. They think I do not hear. It is they who do not hear. They are not listening for My voice, which must be heard in the silence of their heart. A soul who does not put himself in a quiet state will not hear Me. You, My child, have just blocked off your ears and closed your eyes for ten minutes in order to focus wholly on Me. And we are communicating in a supernatural way. But you understand that in order to hear Me, and it has always been this way for you, you must block out the noisy distractions of this world, which grow louder by the day.

I would encourage souls to remove noise from their lives. Turn off the televisions. Turn off the radios. Many conversations are better avoided. In this new silence they will find their heart recollected. In their recollected heart they will find Me, who has been waiting for them.

I am her, dear soul. You need only look into your heart. I ache for you, for your pain, for your loneliness, for your isolation. Each soul feels alone at times and understands that human consolation is empty. They must seek spiritual or heavenly consolation. If you feel a stirring inside, it is your soul, seeking Me. Answer your soul, My dear lost one, for you will find Me waiting and I will solve all of your problems. I can work in you in miraculous ways if only you will allow Me. You have sought other consolations, which have disappointed you. Now try Me. I am here. I love you. I await you.

I want to address holy souls. So often you become discouraged. You do not bear with yourself at all. I, your Jesus, have endless patience with your flaws and weaknesses. YOU must trust Me to forgive you and overlook these human frailties. I am not like a spy, waiting to catch you at bad behavior. Rather, I am your friend. Your greatest advocate. I applaud your small attempts at holiness. Along with the Communion of Saints, I am pulling for you, My holy chosen souls. There is great work to be done. So let us not waste time worrying over our humanity. I don't expect perfection. Please do not expect it from yourself and you won't be discouraged. You must walk with confidence toward Me, always seeking My will. In the smallest details of your day, seek My will. I will make it known to you and, gradually, you will live in a world that is saying "yes" to God. Hunger will disappear, the blackness of sin will recede, and little by little, My goodness will spread to all mankind. This is not impossible. You are skeptical because you live in a world poisoned by skepticism. This skepticism does not come from Me. Be, instead, filled with hope. And certainty. Be certain that the impossible is easy for Me, I could exert My divinity in this world, but I don't want to do that. I want you My chosen ones, to bring about this renewal. That is your mission. Impossible you say? It is not impossible for Me if you allow Me to work through each one of you. And you will be part of the greatest renewal in the history of your world. It is coming. So be of good cheer and do not become discouraged. When you feel hopeless, come to Me and I will infuse you with fresh hope and joy. Your work is important to Me.

Jesus

as given to Anne, a lay apostle

Your thoughts, fused with feeling, become a subjective belief, and according to your belief, is it done unto you.

Having seen the end, you have willed the means to the realization of the end.

Change your thoughts and you change your destiny.

Believe in the power of your subconscious to heal, inspire, strengthen, and prosper you.

By day and by night, I am being prospered in all my interests.

Your true source of wealth consists of the ideas in your mind. You can have an idea worth millions of dollars. Your subconscious will give you the idea you seek.

Joseph Murphy

Choose your own thoughts and make your own decisions.

As within, so without, as above, so below.

There is tremendous power within you. Happiness will come to you when you acquire a sublime confidence in this power. Then, you will make your dreams come true.

You can rise victorious over any defeat and realize the cherished desires of your heart through the marvelous power of your subconscious mind. This is the meaning of "whosoever trusteth in the Lord, happy is he."

You must choose happiness.

Happiness is a habit.

Joseph Murphy

Finally, brethren

whatsoever things are true,

whatsoever things are honest,

whatsoever things are just,

whatsoever things are pure,

whatsoever things are lovely,

whatsoever things are of good report,

if there be any virtue

and if there be any praise,

think on these things.

Philippians 4:8

By constantly dwelling on the thoughts of fear, worry, anger, hate, and failure, you will become very depressed and unhappy. Remember, your life is what your thoughts make of it. The kingdom of happiness is in your thought and feeling.

Happiness is the harvest of a quiet mind. Anchor your thoughts on peace, poise, security and divine guidance, and your mind will be productive of happiness.

There is no block to your happiness. External things are not causative; these are effects, not cause. Take your cue from the only creative principle within you. Your thought is cause, and a new cause produces a new effect. Choose Happiness.

The happiest man is he who brings forth the highest and the best in him. God is the highest and the best in him, for the Kingdom of God is within.

Joseph Murphy

My children of the earth, remain in the awareness that I am with you. You should always know that God, your heavenly Father, is present. In every action, know that I am with you. In every joy and in every suffering, I am with you. I am not just watching, dear ones. I participate with you if I am allowed. To clarify, I live your life on earth intimately united with you if I am welcomed. What benefits does this union with God give you? You make holy and wise decisions. You treat other souls justly. You keep to the path that leads you to spiritual advancement. And most mercifully for you, you serve the Kingdom of God and obtain eternal benefit for your soul. My presence in your life does not guarantee that you will not suffer. Suffering is part of your experience in exile. It means, though that you view suffering with clarity and wisdom. You view suffering as transient, understanding that it passes. You should be at peace with every earthly experience, even the experiences that cause you pain. Children, a reality that you should grasp is that suffering does not pull you away from Me. It can pull you closer if you are far from Me because it pulls you away from things of this world. I created this world for your joy, as I have told you. But the misuse of My gifts can confuse you and lead you away from your path to Me. It is then that I allow suffering for some souls. Do not be angry with Me when you suffer. Unite your suffering to the suffering of My Son and you will find that your ascent to holiness is swift and consoling. Children of God, children of the light, you are Mine. All that occurs in your life has a heavenly purpose. If you do not see the purpose in what you are experiencing now, it is a good sign that you are far from Me and not in communication with Me. Come back to Me and I will explain all of these experiences for you. I want you to have faith, it is true. But I will reveal Myself to you in such a way as to help you to understand what I am attempting to do through you. I am a fair and just God. I will treat all with divine wisdom and mercy if I am asked.

God the Father

as given to Anne, a lay apostle

When you open your eyes in the morning, say to yourself, I choose happiness today. I choose success today. I choose right action today. I choose love and good will for all today. Pour life, love, and interest into this affirmation, and you have chosen happiness.

Give thanks for all your blessings several times a day. Furthermore, pray for the peace, happiness, and prosperity of all members of your family, your associates and all people everywhere.

You must sincerely desire to be happy. Nothing is accomplished without desire. Desire is a wish with wings of imagination and faith. Imagine the fulfillment of your desire, and feel its reality, and it will come to pass.

Happiness comes in answered prayer.

(You have to first know what you want, to ask.)

Joseph Murphy

Souls must understand that Heaven and earth are joined. There is no separation except in the ability of earthly souls to experience Heaven. Brothers and sisters, fellow soldiers for Christ, we are with you. Jesus is with you. There are countless angels with you. Truly, Heaven is with you. Ask for more faith and more faith shall be yours. In order to have confidence and you need confidence, you must understand what we are saying to you. View every day, every event, and every experience as something that you are seeing side by side with us. We are by your side in everything. Why is this so important? We want your view to be similar to our view. Souls discard holiness often because they think they will have to give up too much to be great saints. Do not try to be a great saint. Try to be a little saint because then you will be great, like Therese. Simply rise in the morning and do your duty, keeping Jesus as your goal. If you try to serve quietly in everything you will become a saint in spite of yourself. If something big arises and you are in the habit of serving, you will serve easily, with very little thought. This is where practice and discipline are important. Brothers and sisters, you are to experience a time of change, but you have been prepared if you are following Jesus. If you are not, then you should begin and Jesus will prepare you. Believe me, Philomena, when I tell you that your souls will be protected. Do not fear bodily hardships because these things are fleeting. Be in the habit of denying your body a little every day. Again, this is practice. When you deny yourself, perhaps in fasting, you have not said, "I will never eat again." You have said, "I will not eat for now. I will eat later." It is the same. If you are in a position where your body is being denied something, simply tell yourself that you are being denied at the moment but not forever. You will pray and give thanks to God whatever the circumstances and souls will be saved in great numbers from your prayers of acceptance. There will be the greatest graces available so I do not fear for you because when you experience the times you will have exactly the graces you require. Jesus is so good and He loves us so much! Concentrate on this, my dear friends, and you will not nourish useless fears. We come to provide you with heavenly advice because we have walked your hardships. If you walk with Jesus Christ you have all the power you need, believe me. He will protect you and we, His saints, have the greatest sympathy and love for you. We are truly a family working together. We are working together to rescue souls from the darkness so that they will spend eternity praising our sweet Jesus.

St. Philomena

as given to Anne, a lay apostle

A hateful or resentful thought is a mental poison. You are the only thinker in your universe and your thoughts are creative.

Remember, the other person is not responsible for the way you think about him.

Permit others to differ from you. You can disagree without being disagreeable.

The other person cannot annoy you unless you permit him.

Your thought is creative; you can bless him.

Love is the answer to getting along with others.

Joseph Murphy

The battle is won in the silence of your soul, my dearest friend.

St. Gertrude

To judge is to think, to arrive at a mental verdict or conclusion in your mind. The thought you have about the other person is your thought, because you are thinking it. Your thoughts are creative, therefore, you actually create in your own experience what you think and feel about the other person. It is also true that the suggestion you give to another, you give to yourself because your mind is the creative medium.

This is why it is said, "For with what judgment ye judge, ye shall be judged." When you know this law and the way your subconscious mind works, you are careful to think, feel, and act right toward the other.

Mind is then the source of all things, in the sense that the activity of mind is the initial cause of all things coming into being. This is because the primal source of all things is a corresponding thought in the Universal Mind. It is the essence of a thing that constitutes its being and the activity of mind is the cause by which the essence takes form.

An idea is a thought conceived in the mind and this rational form of the thought is the root of form in the sense that this form of thought is the initial formal expression which, acting upon substance, causes it to assume form.

There can be nothing except as there is an idea, or ideal form, engendered in the Mind. Such ideas, acting upon the Universal, engender corresponding forms.

These verses teach you about the emancipation of man and reveal to you the solution to your individual problems.

Joseph Murphy

Wish for the other what you wish for yourself. This is the key to harmonious human relations.

To understand all is to forgive all.

You cannot be hurt by criticism when you know that you are master of your thoughts, reactions, and emotions. This gives you the opportunity to pray and bless the other, thereby blessing yourself.

When you pray for guidance and right action, take what comes.

Joseph Murphy

*On The Bright Side*

Dear brothers and sisters, how brave you are to read these words with faith. There must be a great push now for detachment. Try to concentrate on heavenly thoughts and heavenly goals, even while you remain in the world. In this way you will detach from the world more effectively and you will see the fruits of these words in your soul. Words are simply words, as you know, until they begin to impact behaviors and habits and, of course, souls, If you ingest these words quietly, they will take root in your souls and all manner of beautiful and exotic blooms will begin to form. The graces are there my friends. Heaven needs only a willing spirit who will put herself in silence so that these graces can take root. Do not let these graces be wasted. Sometimes souls take the graces and admire their beauty. They correctly assess the worth of these heavenly gifts. But it is one thing to admire the work of a beautiful blanket or quilt. It is another to wrap yourself in it and allow it to warm you which is its true function. The true function of these words and their accompanying graces is growth. We want to facilitate change in your souls. Your souls must stretch now and to do that you must minimize the attention you pay to the world and maximize the attention you pay to your faith. Jesus is with you, awaiting your notice so that He can take your hand and begin a walk of union with you. Do not hold back from Him because you limit Him when you do. Give Him everything. Ask Him all throughout the day what you can do for Him. Do this fearlessly, understanding that if He gives you something to do, He will give you every grace necessary to do it. You need fear nothing, little souls. I have the greatest of love and understanding for you, as do we all. We repeat that so you will be reminded and remember to call upon us in your moments of difficulty or fear. Many things can cause fear but usually if you are aligned with Jesus your fears are easily managed. You will know when you are neglecting your prayers, my friends, because fears will begin to creep back into your minds. When I felt fear I began to praise God. In this way I turned the fear into a prayer and trained myself to allow Jesus to eradicate my fears. He always did. Again I say you should ask for the graces as the graces are there. You should not feel that you cannot experience the joy of Jesus because you are afraid. That would tell you that something is wrong and quite possibly you must simply pray more. We speak in simple words because Heaven never seeks to confuse. Confusion does not come from Heaven so you understand that it comes from the enemy of Heaven. Confusion, like fear, is a symptom of the enemy's presence. Expect to struggle with these little crosses at times and you will not be alarmed or pay too much attention. When you find the cross of confusion or fear becoming heavy or quite noticeable, flee to your duty and wrap yourself in prayer. We all carried those crosses, dear friends. We understand and will help you. Suffering from these things does not mean you do not serve Christ well. On the contrary, it would be a nice thing to walk in blissful peace at all times but if you are a follower of Christ this will not be your experience, believe me. I say this with a light heart because we in Heaven are so joyful at the beautiful and brave way that we accepted such crosses. It is like running a race against yourself and winning. We look back and say, "That fear could have distracted me from serving Christ but I kept my eyes on Christ and did not let it. Good for me." You will say this too and you too will be joyful at what you accomplish.

St. Gertrude the Great

as given to Anne, a lay apostle

"The real cause of alcoholism is negative and destructive thinking. 'As a man thinketh in his heart, so is he'"

When fear knocks at the door of your mind, let faith in God and all things good open the door.

Joseph Murphy

Do the things you are afraid to do, and the death of fear is certain.

Ralph Waldo Emerson

When fear arises, there immediately comes with it a desire for something opposite to the thing feared. Place your attention on the thing immediately desired. Get absorbed and engrossed in your desire, knowing that he subjective always overturns the objective.

Move mentally to the opposite.

Joseph Murphy

Brothers and sisters, I have come with words of encouragement for you. The words and thoughts in these messages are an example of the great mercy of our God in Heaven. You will be so grateful that you served when you are called to come home. There is not regret like the regret you will have if you say "no" to Jesus during this time. We know Jesus, both as man and as God. He is all love. He is all kindness. He is all encouraging and uplifting. Jesus never leaves you feeling saddened, unless you are walking away without determination to serve Him. Spend time with Him always because you will always feel refreshed and determined. I got all of my courage from Jesus Christ personally, whether I was in His presence or not. Truly, I felt united to Him because I allowed Him to be united to me. You can do that, too. That is one of the opportunities you have during these days especially. Jesus wants to work through you. To do that, He must be with you. Would you like to walk with Christ, constantly united to Him and in His presence? You can. Just make the decision and ask Him to be with you. Then, when you have done that do not ignore Him or treat Him with such familiarity that you forget Him. He is your closest friend. He is your ever-present advisor. Think of your current problems. What does Jesus say about these problems? What is His opinion? What does He want you to do about these struggles or conflicts? If you do not know the answer, you are not doing it right. Spend time in silence with Him and ask Him. I lived like this. All day long I said, "Jesus, what would You like me to do? Jesus, how are You going to handle this?" He will give you the answer and you will reach His goal of behaving as another Christ in the world. Brothers and sisters, we do not wish to bore you by repeating lessons. But because we are also experienced with humanity, we know that often you must learn the same lessons over and over. Repetition and practice bring perfection. We know that. We learned it the old-fashioned way which was by making the same mistakes and relearning these important lessons. Jesus is with you. Jesus will never leave you. Do not be afraid and do not make any decisions without His counsel. If you are fearful, you are doing something wrong. If you are panicking, you are doing something wrong. If you feel dislike for most of your brothers and sisters you are doing something wrong. And if you feel you are better than most of your fellow apostles, you are in trouble. I am making a joke so do not be too serious. I speak of such serious things that I feel I must lighten your mood. In all of this, you should feel a sense of liberation because when Jesus is leading your life you are liberated. Can you imagine the burden of doing it all by yourself? Imagine the fear of making mistakes if you put yourself back in charge. Truly, once you begin walking with Christ it would be very traumatic to break away on your own again. The world would once again become the frightening place it is for non-believers. I love you so passionately, my friends. We all do. We are so eager to help you. We can give you the most beautiful counsel. Talk to us often and we will find ways to help you and obtain beautiful gifts of grace from our God. Peace be with you, dear fellow apostles, You are in the greatest of company.

St. Matthew the apostle

as given to Anne, a lay apostle

Fear is a negative thought in your mind. Supplant it with a constructive thought.

Confidence is greater than fear.

Nothing is more powerful than faith in God and the good.

Fear is man's greatest enemy.

Love casts out fear.

Give your immediate attention and devotion to your desire

which is the opposite of your fear.

This is the love which casts out fear.

The things you fear do not exist except as thoughts in your mind. Thoughts are creative. Think good and good follows.

Joseph Murphy

Wisdom is an awareness of the tremendous spiritual powers in your subconscious mind and the knowledge of how to apply these powers to lead a full and happy life.

Getting older can be the beginning of a glorious, fruitful, active and most productive life pattern, better than you have ever experienced. Believe this, expect it, and your subconscious will bring it to pass.

You grow old when you lose interest in life, when you cease to dream, to hunger after new truths, and to search for new worlds to conquer.

When your mind is open to new ideas, new interests and when you raise the curtain and let in the sunshine and inspiration of new truths of life and the universe, you will be young and vital.

You must be a producer.

Nothing can disturb you but your own thoughts.

Joseph Murphy

What you call the aging process is only change. It is to be welcomed joyfully and gladly as each phase of human life is a step forward on the path which has on end. Man has powers which transcend his bodily powers. He has senses which transcend his five physical senses.

You are as young as you think you are.

Life is, and we are here to express it in all its beauty and glory.

The suggestions, statements, or threats of other persons have no power. The power is within you, and when your thoughts are focused on that which is good, then God's power is with your thoughts of good.

There is only one Creative Power, and it moves as Harmony. There are no divisions or quarrels in it. Its' source is love. This is why God's power is with your thoughts of good.

Joseph Murphy

I wish to speak to My children about heaven. The coming of My Kingdom is the coming of heaven or the expansion of heaven to earth. This is part of My plan and this is what the future holds for My children. Can you see it, dear ones? True happiness can be found only in the union of a soul's will to the divine will. When your will is united to the divine will, there is no conflict, no struggle. Only a very few find such union on earth. The seeking of this union is the path to holiness that you follow in your obedience to My commandments. You are making decisions. You are moving forward along the road. You are making corrections. This is the process. At times in the history of mankind, most souls on earth were moving in the general direction of heaven. At this time, most souls are languishing along the way. Many are wasting their time on earth and are not coming in this direction at all. In this way, souls are lost. As a God of mercy, I send all manner of signs and warnings. In this time, however, most of My signs are being ignored. Such is the level of distraction, that My souls no sooner see a sign and experience My call, then they allow themselves to be distracted and pulled back into the world. Children, pay attention. You must be disciplined if you are to remain on the path to salvation. And believe Me when I say that all other roads lead nowhere. My children belong with each other, loving Me. Hear my call of love, now, while I can offer you a soft and gentle transition to holiness. There is coming a time, as you have been told, when the transition will only be possible with violence. It will be a shock to you if you do not respond now. Children, if you are not following My words, if you are not united with Me, if you do not acknowledge and respect My dominion over both you and your world, you are going to be uncomfortable and frightened. These times are over. My time is coming. There will be gladness, it is true. It is what My children have prayed for. But change is difficult for those without a firm understanding and belief in the next world. If you were asked to hand your life to Me this day, and account for it fully, how would you feel? Would you feel calm? Would you feel confident that while you have made mistakes, you have done your best and can offer Me a fair trade for your eternal reward? Could you even say, "God, I have wasted much of my time here on earth but I see that You are the Creator and I bow before You?" That is all that is necessary for your salvation, child, but you are going to wish that you had a small bit of something to give Me. You might give Me your years parenting your children. You might offer Me your service in your job or your obedience and respect for your parents. You might give Me your patience with sickness or depression. You might say, "God, I have risen every day and tried not to be dishonest or hurtful to others, despite my pain and misery." To all of these things, and to nearly every life that holds dignity and some measure of effort to be honest, I will say, "Welcome. Well done. It is over now and you are safe and loved." I will hold you against Me and heal all of your wounds and pain. You will be lovingly prepared to enter into the Kingdom. Children, do not be afraid of leaving this world and entering the next. I will be there, waiting to receive each one of you.

God the Father

as given to Anne, a lay apostle

The secret of youth is love, joy, inner peace, and laughter. "In Him there is fullness of joy. In Him there is no darkness at all."

The fruits of old age are love, joy, peace, patience, gentleness, goodness, faith, meekness, and temperance.

You are a young as you think you are.

You are as strong as you think you are.

You are a useful as you think you are.

You are as young as your thoughts.

Become a producer, not a prisoner of society.

Joseph Murphy

*On The Bright Side*

Faith is the bird that feels the light and sings when the dawn is still dark.

Rabindranath Tagore

You are a son of Infinite Life which knows no end.

You are a child of Eternity.

You are wonderful.

You are loved.

Joseph Murphy

We become what we think about. What is your vision of your future?

We grow into our expectations. As you think – so shall you become.

Earl Nightingale

As the wheel follows the ox behind, so we become what we think about.

Earl Nightingale

*On The Bright Side*

All children of this earth, hear My call. Your God communicates with you in all majesty. I will do anything to save a soul and I have great power. The only thing I cannot overturn is your free will. If a soul chooses darkness over Me, there is nothing I can do, for your free will is My gift to you and the Father will never take back a gift once given. It would be alien to the very nature of God. But you will return to Me. Return now, in your heart. I am speaking to you in this way because I want you to be in heaven with Me for your eternity. Is anything above this a priority? Could there possible be anything more important? No. There is nothing more important than this one simple thing to gain heaven. Put aside all else right now. Sit with Me as I minister to your heart and prepare you to meet Me. I want only your salvation. I am sending the greatest graces through My words to you and as God I would have you back in My heart from this moment on. Will you remain with Me, dearest soul? Do not go away from Me again. You have sampled the world's offerings and you have been left unloved and in darkness. I offer you all that is light and good. I offer you safety and confidence. I will nourish you in times of hunger and console you in sadness. You need nothing, only Me. There is no reason to languish. Your God has called you by name. Come to Me.

God the Father

as given to Anne, a lay apostle

Thoughts of courage, power, and inspiration will eventually take root, and as this takes place, you will see life in a new light.

Life will have a new meaning for you. You will be reconstructed and filled with joy, confidence, hope, and energy.

You will see opportunities to which you were heretofore blind. You will recognize possibilities which before had no meaning for you.

The thoughts with which you have been impregnated are radiated to those around you, and they in turn help you onward and upward; you attract to yourself new associates, and this in turn changes your environment; so that by this simple exercise of thought, you change not only yourself, but your environment, circumstances, and conditions.

Every thought brings into action certain physical tissue – parts of the brain, nerve, or muscles. This produces an actual physical change in the construction of the tissue. Therefore, it is only necessary to have a certain number of thoughts on a given subject in order to bring about a compete change in your physical organization

Charles Haanel

Thoughts of anger, hatred, fear, jealousy, worry, etc., act directly on the secretions causing an actual poison in the system which in time will destroy the body unless they are overcome with love, harmony, joy, faith, etc. Constructive thoughts and love is the strongest of all.

We are told by the greatest of teachers that the fundamental or foundation law of our being is love. Love God, love your neighbor, love yourself, love your enemy, love everybody and everything. No one can afford to hate because hate always destroys the hater. It is said that "Whom the gods would destroy, they first make angry."

Prosperity is a harmonious, creative state of being. Creative law will overcome every kind of in-harmony, whether it be financial, physical, mental, moral, or social.

Thoughts of prosperity, love, joy, and happiness also act upon the heart, causing good circulation and a healthy body. There is much truth in the saying, "A merry heart doeth good like a medicine."

Charles Haanel

If you send thoughts of health, love, and prosperity, they will return to you multiplied like the seed you sow in your garden.

Send out destructive thoughts, they also return to you multiplied like weeds. You reap what you sow.

You have seen that when any thought, idea or purpose finds its way in the subconscious through the emotions, the sympathetic nervous system takes up the thought, idea or purpose, and carries it to every part of the body, thus converting the idea, thought, or purpose into an actual experience in your life.

Mind is then the source of all things, in the sense that the activity of mind is the initial cause of all things coming into being. This is because the primal source of all things is a corresponding thought in the Universal Mind. It is the essence of a thing that constitutes its being and the activity of mind is the cause by which the essence takes form.

An idea is a thought conceived in the mind and this rational form of the thought is the root of form in the sense that this form of thought is the initial formal expression which, acting upon substance, causes it to assume form.

There can be nothing except as there is an idea, or ideal form, engendered in the Mind. Such ideas, acting upon the Universal, engender corresponding forms.

Charles Haanel

## Peter Bell

He moved among the vales and streams,
In the green wood and hollow dell;
They were his dwelling night and day
But Nature ne'er could find the way
Into the heart of Peter Bell.

In Vain through every changing year,
Did Nature lead him as before,
A primrose by the river's brim,
A yellow primrose was to him,
And it was nothing more

Wordsworth

He who does not understand your silence will probably not understand your words.

Every man is a damn fool for at least five minutes every day; wisdom consists in not exceeding the limit.

Art is not a thing; it is a way.

To avoid criticism, do nothing, say nothing, and be nothing.

Life in abundance comes only through great love.

Responsibility is the price of freedom.

The line between failure and success is so fine that we scarcely know when we pass; so fine that we are often on the line and do not know it.

The sculptor produces the beautiful statue by chipping away such parts of the marble block as are not needed – it is a process of elimination.

Elbert Hubbard

A little more persistence, a little more effort
and what seemed hopeless failure may turn to glorious success.

God will not look you over for medals, degrees, or diplomas, but for scars.

Character is the result of two things:
Mental attitude and the way we spend our time.

Know what you want to do, hold the thought firmly, and do every day what should be done, and every sunset will see you that much nearer to your goal.

It does not take much strength to do things, but it requires a great deal of strength to decide what to do.

Happiness is a habit – cultivate it.

Elbert Hubbard

*On The Bright Side*

One machine can do the work of fifty ordinary men.

No machine can do the work of one extraordinary man.

We work to become, not to acquire.

Fear is the thought of admitted inferiority.

A man is not paid for a head and hands but for using them.

Every tyrant who ever lived believed in freedom for himself.

Fear clogs; faith liberates.

The thing we fear we bring to pass.

Elbert Hubbard

My child, for so long I have watched you. In some deep area of your soul, you knew I was there with you. I choose to be more active in your life now. I choose to lead you more directly, if you will allow Me. I want My children to be united with Me, but also with each other. I require a legion of souls who are living in union with Me, their God, and who are responding to My directives. Children, along with My Son, and Mary, His mother, I am giving you every assurance of your welcome. You are being guided in an unprecedented fashion and this guidance will continue. We will shepherd you through all difficulties. Many souls think that they do not have to return to Me now because they will have time later. They procrastinate. Children, this is not what I want. This is not what I am asking of you. I say, "Enough." Come to Me now. In order to enter heaven, you must accept Jesus, My Son. You know this. Do this now. Do I ask this of you so that I will have greater glory? Am I a selfish God who seeks My own comfort? Children, surely you know this is not the case. If your God is calling out to you, if your God is sending all manner of signs and warnings, you must assume and understand that your God is trying to spare you difficulty and upset. I want My children at peace. I want My children to be detached from the world, understanding that the heavenly Kingdom is their home and their destination. If you are on a journey, a long journey, and suddenly you arrive at your destination, do you not celebrate? Of course you do, children. You do not say, "No thank you, we do not wish to arrive at our goal. We prefer to continue traveling." The longer and more difficult the journey, the more relieved you feel at its end. Such celebration greets the end of a journey. Can you imagine, children, what celebrations will be waiting for you when you reach the end of your journey on earth and arrive home in your Kingdom? You will not be disappointed. Your God, I, your Father, have prepared the most glorious banquet with everything that is beautiful in creation. Children earthly delights are nothing in comparison. Do not cling to the things of this earth. You will leave them eventually. Your humanity dictates that your time on earth is finite. Dearest, the earth itself is finite. Only I am infinite. If you plan to choose Me eventually, choose Me now. If somewhere in your heart you recognize that I am your God and you are My creature, come to Me now. I want your soul to be preserved and protected.

God the Father

as given to Anne, a lay apostle

Your mind is a 'thought factory.' It's a busy factory producing countless thoughts in one day. Production in your thought factory is under the charge of two foremen, one of whom we will call Mr. Triumph, and the other Mr. Defeat.

Mr. Triumph is in charge of manufacturing positive thoughts. He specializes in producing reasons why you can, why you're qualified, why you will.

The other foreman, Mr. Defeat produces negative depreciating thoughts. He is your expert in developing reasons why you can't, why you're weak, why you're inadequate. His specialty is the 'why you will fail' chain of thought.

Both Mr. Triumph and Mr. Defeat are intensely obedient. They snap to attention immediately. All you need to do to signal ether foreman is to give the slightest mental beck-and-call. If the signal is positive, Mr. Triumph will step forward and go to work. Likewise a negative signal brings Mr. Defeat.

…Now, the more work you give either of these foremen, the stronger he becomes. If Mr. Defeat is given more work to do, he adds personnel and takes up more space in your mind. Eventually he will take over the entire thought manufacturing division, and virtually all thought will be of a negative nature.

The only thing to do is fire Mr. Defeat. You don't need him. You don't want him around telling you that you can't, you're not up to it, you'll fail, and so on. Mr. Defeat won't help you get where you want to go, so boot him out.

Use Mr. Triumph 100 percent of the time. When any thought enters your mind, ask Mr. Triumph to go work for you. He'll show you how you can succeed.

…Walk in. The door to success is open wider than ever before. Put yourself on record now that you are going to join that select group that is getting what it wants from life.

David Schwartz

Here is the first step towards success. It is a basic step. It can't be avoided. Step One: Believe in yourself, believe you can succeed.

Here are the three guides to acquire and strengthen the power of belief:

1) Think Success, don't think failure. At work, in your home, substitute success thinking for failure thinking. When you face a difficult situation think, "I'll win", not "I'll probably lose." When you compete with someone else think, "I'm equal to the best." When opportunity appears, think "I can do it", never "I can't." Let the master thought "I will succeed" dominate your thinking process. Thinking success conditions your mind to create plans that produce success.

2) Remind yourself regularly that you are better than you think you are. Successful people are not Superman. Success does not require a super intellect. Nor is there anything mystical about success. And success isn't based on luck. Successful people are just ordinary folks who have developed belief in themselves and what they do. Never – yes never – sell yourself short.

3) Believe Big. The size of your success is determined by the size of your belief. Think little goals and expect little achievements. Think big goals and win big success. Remember this too! Big ideas and big plans are often easier – certainly no more difficult – than small ideas and small plans.

David Schwartz

*On The Bright Side*

Positive attitude,

Like people,

Be an idea person – not a fact person.


Attitude is more important than Intelligence.

The <u>ability</u> to <u>think</u> is more important than facts.


Action cures fear. (Indecision and postponement, on the other hand, fertilizes fear.) When we face tough problems we stay mired in the muck, until we take action. Hope is a start. <u>But hope needs action to win victories</u>.


What kind of action can I take to conquer my fear? Isolate your fear. Then take appropriate action. Take action promptly – be decisive.


To think confidently, act confidently.


Motions are the precursors of emotions.


David Schwartz

*On The Bright Side*

## Five Procedures

1) Action cures fear.

2) Put only positive thought in your memory bank. Refuse to recall unpleasant events or situation.

3) Put people in perspective. They are more alike than different.

4) Do what your conscience says is right.

5) Make everything about you say "I'm confident, really confident."

We do not think in words and phrases. We think only in pictures and/or images.

When you speak or write, you are, in a sense, a projector showing movies in the minds of others. And the pictures you create determine how you and others react.

David Schwartz

Children of the world, you are precious to Me. Each one of you was created with infinite forethought and love. Each one of your characteristics is an act of My mercy. "My God" you may say, 'not all of my characteristics are lovable." I know that, My child. You have certain flaws to overcome. Do you think I love you less for them? Is not a favored plaything often marked? Does it not bear the signs of a child's love and interest? Children, I love you in all of your imperfection. I love you with all of the scars and marks you carry as the result of your flaws and mistakes. They mean nothing to Me in the sense that I did not make you to be perfect. I made you to overcome your weaknesses, and utilizing your free will, to choose Me. I made you to assist each other. I created you to adorn heaven and, little one, I want you here with Me. There is a place I have prepared. It is for only you. You have a home here forever and I would have you prepare to complete your journey. Do I frighten you? I do not intend to frighten you and it is not to frighten that I come. On the contrary, dear ones, I come to explain to each of you that you are always one breath away from eternity. It is the same for each soul who has ever been on earth. From this moment to the next, your journey may be complete. I will decide. In Times past, souls would remind themselves of this fact and use those thoughts to keep themselves detached from the world. Because of the many gifts and advances I have given and allowed, My children delude themselves into thinking I am passe and that My time has gone. Dear ones, have you ever heard of anything so absurd and arrogant? You may say, "Surely not God. No soul breathing the air You have given us would think that way. And yet they do. If you are a soul who thinks you have no need for your divine Creator pause for a moment. Stop breathing. I want you to realize that at any time, I can will this. Such is My power. Do not think you are independent of Me. If not for Me, you would cease to exist. I am God. I am omnipotent. My own know Me. You are My own and I want your allegiance.

God the Father

as given to Anne, a lay apostle

*On The Bright Side*

The fact is that the greatest discovery of all ages is that of physical science that all things apparently have their source in the invisible, intangible, ether.

"Whosoever…shall not doubt in his heart, but shall believe that what he said cometh to pass, he shall have it."

When we know that certain potent ideas exist in the invisible mind expressions, named by science both 'ether' and 'space' and that we have been provided with the mind to lay hold of them, it is easy to put the law into action through thought and word and deed.

The spiritual substance from which comes all visible wealth is never depleted. It is right with you all the time and responds to your faith in it and your demands on it.

It is not affected by our ignorant talk of hard ties, though we are affected because our thoughts and words govern our demonstration. The unfailing resource is always ready to give. It has no choice in the matter; it must give, for that is its nature. Pour your living words of faith into the omnipresent substance, and you will be prospered though all the banks in the world close their doors. Turn the great energy of your thinking toward "plenty" ideas, and you will have plenty regardless of what men about you are saying or doing.

Substance is first given form in the mind and as it becomes manifest it goes through a threefold activity. In laying hold of substance in the mind and bringing it into manifestation, we play a most important part. We do it according to our decree. "Thou shalt decree a thing, and it shall be established unto thee." We are always decreeing, sometimes consciously, often unconsciously, and with every thought and word we are increasing or diminishing the threefold activity of substance. The resulting manifestation conforms to our thought, 'as he thinketh within himself, so is he.'

There is a kingdom of abundance in all things, and it may be found by those who seek it and are willing to comply with its laws. Jesus said that it is hard for a rich man to enter into the Kingdom of Heaven. This does not mean that it is hard because of his wealth, for the poor man gets in no faster and no easier. It is not money but the thoughts men hold about money, its source, its ownership, and its use, that keep them out of the Kingdom.

Men's thoughts about money are like their thoughts about all possessions; they believe that things coming out of the earth are theirs to claim and control as individual property and may be hoarded away and depended on, regardless of how much other men may be in need of them. The same belief is prevalent among both rich and poor, and even if the two classes were suddenly to change places, the inequalities of wealth would not be remedied. Only a fundamental change in the thoughts of wealth could do that.

Charles Fillmore

## Strategic Planning

1) Where are you now? Starting point.

2) Where would you like to be?

3) How did you get to where you are today?

4) What can you do now, to get to where you want to go from where you are?

What should you be doing more of?

What should you be doing less of?

What should you start doing that you are not doing?

What should you stop doing altogether?

Based on writings of Jack Canfield

## Goals

Every day, open notebook and write down a list of your 10-15 most important goals, without referring to your previous list. You r goals must be listed in the positive, present, and personal tense. "I earn …a month by …"

Set deadlines.

After each goal, write down at least three activities that you could take immediately to achieve that goal, also in present, positive and personal tense. "1) I… every day in advance. 2) I start immediately on…. 3) I concentrate single mindedly on..."

After one month, write out 15 goals on index cards and carry them with you everywhere. Review each of your goals one at a time, twice a day.

Visualize yourself following steps to achieve goal.

Review your goals first thing in the morning and last thing at night.

Make a list of the tasks for the following day the night before.

Visualize your goals with: frequency, duration, vividness, and intensity.

Use mental rehearsal before an event.

Jack Canfield

God draws into your life the people, circumstances and resources that you need to achieve your goals.

Vision – visualize and focus on the goals that are most important to you.

Visualize successful experiences – feed your mind with positive images.

Dwell on the quality you want to have and imagine that you have it already. Imagine yourself practicing that quality and/or virtue

Relax deeply and see the desired result.

Brian Tracy

When you have clear goals – written and rewritten, visualized and emotionalized, you trigger your conscious, subconscious, and superconscious minds into generating a continuous flow of ideas for goal attainment.

Mind Storming – At the top of the page, write your goal or problem in the form of a question. The simpler and more specific the question, the better. Each of your answers should be written in the personal, positive and present tense.

Generate at least 20 answers to the question. The last ten will be difficult but will exercise your brain to be more creative. Don't quit until you have at least twenty answers. Often the last idea is inspirational. Go over your answers and select at least one answer that you can take immediately towards solving the problem or reaching the goal. You can multiply the effectiveness by taking the best answer and writing it as a question on a new blank sheet of paper and generating 20 more answers.

Do Mind Storming each morning after you have written your goals.

Use on every goal – do one per morning. Do the same goal for several weeks if it's big enough.

1) Define problem clearly.

2) Ask: What are all the possible causes of this problem?

3) What are all the possible solutions? What is another solution?

4) What must this solution accomplish?

5) Assign specific responsibility or take responsibility yourself for implementing the solution.

Think on paper. Write it down.

Brian Tracy

Big thinkers are specialists in creating positive, forward looking, optimistic pictures in their own minds and in the minds of others. To think big we must use words and phrases which produce big, positive mental images.

Big thinkers train themselves to see not what is, but what can be. Visualization adds value to everything. A big thinker always visualizes what can be done in the future. He isn't stuck with the present.

The price tag the world puts on us is just about identical to the one we put on ourselves. See what can be.

Ask yourself"

1) How can I add value to this…a thing has value in proportion to the ideas for using it.

2) Practice adding value to people – what can I do to help them become more effective. Remember, to bring out the best in a person, you must first visualize his best.

3) Practice adding value to yourself. Visualize yourself not as you are now, but as you can be.

David Schwartz

My children, I have called you. I have pleaded with you. I have explained to you why you must return to Me. You should come back to My heart and remain with Me now in the spirit of loyalty and love. If you have a difficult time and feel pulled by the world, know that this conflict is your portion. You are earning your heaven by your detachment from the earth. You are showing Me that you are trying to become worthy of heaven and that you are preparing yourself. Children, the smallest efforts on your part will be rewarded in a truly unprecedented manner. The children of the world have been led far astray at this time but I come now to bring them back. I do not judge you at this time. I love you. I come to you in all patience and understanding. Come to Me in the spirit of obedience and you will move swiftly on a straight path that leads directly to holiness. No fear now, My children. I have only good intentions for you. Be at peace in everything. Your God will protect you and preserve you.

God the Father

as given to Anne, a lay apostle

www.ingramcontent.com/pod-product-compliance
Lightning Source LLC
Chambersburg PA
CBHW071520040426
42444CB00008B/1728